Mel Bay Presents

THE
AMERICAN HISTORY
SONGBOOK

By Jerry Silverman

Cover illustration by Greg Ragland.

A Note From Jerry Silverman

Our country's strong,
Our country's young,
And its greatest songs are still unsung.
—The Ballad for Americans

That may be so, but still we have created some pretty good ones over the course of the past 250 or so years. We've sung of the good times and the bad, the triumphs and defeats, the hopes and disappointments. . . . Mostly we've sung about people — real people and how they feel.

The songs in this collection trace the history of this nation from its Colonial beginnings on the New England shore and follow the movement of its people in their inexorable southern and western expansion. Then, when the transcontinental railroad linked the two great oceans, the people and their songs turned their attention to the rest of the world and its battles.

In a half dozen foreign wars over the past century, songs followed the flag — sometimes supportive of our efforts, sometimes not. At home during roughly the same period, other battles were being fought, and songs sung, on behalf of the rights of women, labor and blacks.

Perhaps the greatest concentrated outpouring of song occurred during the Civil War. Since it was a *civil* war, soldiers and songwriters on both sides expressed themselves in the same language musically and in terms of sentiment (albeit with opposing points of view as to the right and wrong of the conflict). Only a very few of those thousands of songs could be represented here.

A musical thread woven throughout our entire history as a republic is the presidential election campaign song. Although memorable campaign songs in recent elections are hard to find, the 19th century and the first decades of the 20th did produce innumerable musical winners — even though their heroes were sometimes losers!

If there is a point of view expressed in this collection, it is that of that elusive subject — the "common" man and woman. Each singer has stood up and let out a yell, a cry, a moan, a laugh. . . . Carl Sandburg said it best in *The People, Yes:*

The hallelujah chorus
Forever shifting its star soloist.

Contents

Colonial America
17th and 18th Centuries

An Invitation to North America

In 18th-century England the wonders of "North Americay" were sung from penny broadsides — wordsheets featuring new compositions set to familiar tunes. This song was based on the song "Liliburlero" by Henry Purcell, which was written in 1687.

Come all you bold Brit–ons, where–ev–er you be, I would have you draw near and lis – ten to me. The times they get hard – er in Eng–land ev –'ry day; It is much bet– ter liv – ing in North A– me – ri – cay.

There is many a family of late that has gone
Away to New York, father, mother and son;
Let us likewise follow and make no delay,
For 'tis much cheaper living in North Americay.

The farmers in England sell their corn so dear,
They do what they can to starve the poor here.
They send it to France, which sure is not right,
To feed other nations that against us do fight.

Why do we stay here for to be their slaves,
When in Nova Scotia we can do as we please;
For who'd work in England for ten pence a day,
When we can get four shillings in North Americay.

The landlords in England do raise the lands high,
It forces some farmers abroad for to fly;
If times grow no better, I'll venture to say,
Poor men had better go to North Americay.

Observe then good people what to you I've told,
What a plague is in England by short weight of gold.
With bad silver and halfpence, believe what I say,
There's nothing of this in North Americay.

The priests in England come into the field,
They tithe as they please, you dare not but yield,
This is a great hardship, you believe, I dare say.
But we'll have no taxes in North Americay.

There's many a farmer you very well know,
That went to New York but a few years ago,
Have bought land and houses; who now would here stay,
But go and make fortunes in North Americay.

Manufactures in England are grown very bad,
For weavers and combers no work's to be had.
But let's go abroad, I dare venture to say,
They'll find us employment in North Americay.

So here's a health to George our gracious king,
I hope none will take amiss the song that I sing;
Then lads and lasses now come away,
And ship yourselves to North Americay.

The Distressed Damsel

The realities of life in colonial America were often quite harsh—particularly for indentured servants, who owed their employers years of labor to pay for their passage over.

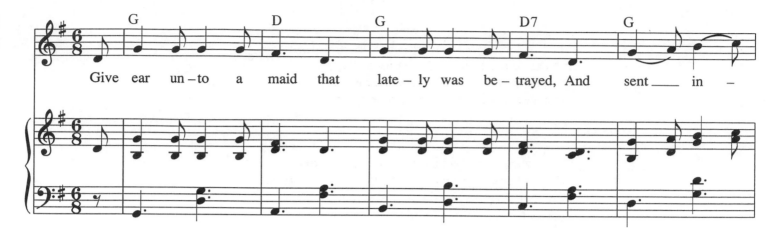

Give ear un–to a maid that late–ly was be – trayed, And sent ___ in –

to ___ Vir – gin – ny, O; In brief I shall de – clare, what

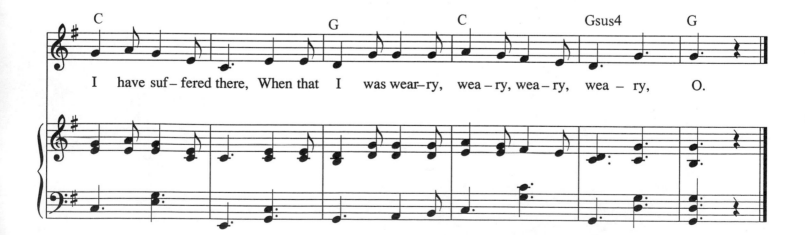

I have suf–fered there, When that I was wear–ry, wea–ry, wea–ry, wea – ry, O.

When that first I came
To this land of fame,
Which is called Virginny, O.
The axe and the hoe
Have brought my overthrow.
When that I was weary, etc.

Five years served I
Under Master Guy,
In the land of Virginny, O.
Which made me for to know
Sorrow, grief and woe,
When that I was weary, etc.

When my Dame says, "Go,"
Then I must do so,
In the land of Virginny, O.
When she sits at meat,
Then I have none to eat,
When that I was weary, etc.

The clothes that I brought in
They are worn very thin,
In the land of Virginny, O'.
Which makes me for to say,
Alas and well-a-day,
When that I was weary, etc.

Instead of beds of ease,
To lie down when I please,
In the land of Virginny, O:
Upon a bed of straw,
I lay down full of woe,
When that I was weary, etc.

Then the spider she,
Daily waits on me,
In the land of Virginny, O;
Round about my bed
She spins her tender web,
When that I am weary, etc.

So soon as it is day,
To work I must away,
In the land of Virginny, O·
Then my dame she knocks
With her tinder-box,
When that I was weary, etc.

I have played my part,
Both at plow and cart,
In the land of Virginny, O:
Billets from the wood,
Upon my back they load,
When that I was weary, etc.

Instead of drinking beer,
I drink the water clear,
In the land of Virginny, O:
Which makes me pale and wan,
Do all that e'er I can,
When that I was weary, etc.

If my dame says, "Go!"
I dare not say no,
In the land of Virginny, O:
The water from the spring
Upon my head I bring,
When that I was weary, etc.

When the child doth cry,
I must sing, "By a by,"
In the land of Virginny, O.
No rest that I can have,
Whilst I am here a slave,
When that I was weary, etc.

A thousand woes beside,
That I do here abide,
In the land of Virginny, O:
In misery I spend
My time that hath no end,
When that I was weary, etc.

Then let maids beware,
All by my ill-fare,
In the land of Virginny, O:
Be sure you stay at home,
For if you do here come,
You all will be weary, etc.

But if it be my chance,
Homewards to advance,
From the land of Virginny, O:
If that I once more
Land on English shore,
I'll no more be weary,
Weary, weary, weary, O.

From an original indenture in the Hingham Historical Society

A New England Ballad

A disillusioned 18th-century British immigrant returns to England where he dispels a few myths concerning New England.

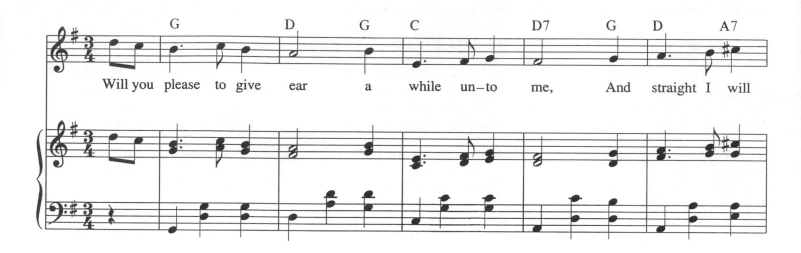

Will you please to give ear a while un—to me, And straight I will

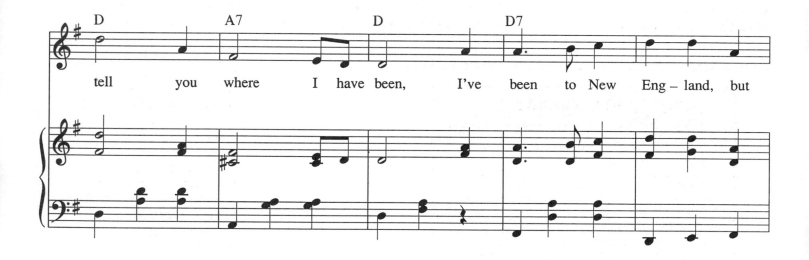

tell you where I have been, I've been to New Eng – land, but

now have come o'er, I think they shall catch me go thith – er no

more, I think they shall catch me go thith – er no more.

Before I went thither, Lord how folks did tell,
How wishes did grow and how birds did dwell,
All one 'mongst t'other in the wood and the water,
I thought that was true, but I found no such matter. (2)

When first I did land, they 'mazed me quite,
And 'twas of all days on a Saturday night;
I wondered to see strange buildings were there,
'Twas all like the standings at Woodbury Fair. (2)

Well, that night I slept 'til near prayer time,
Next morning I wondered I heard no bells chime;
At which I did ask and the reason I found
'Twas because they had ne'er a bell in the town. (2)

At last being warned, to church we repaired,
Where I did think certain we should have some prayers;
But the parson there no such matter did teach,
They scorned to pray for all one could preach. (2)

The first thing they did, a psalm they did sing,
I plucked out my Psalm-book I with me did bring;
And tumbled to seek it, 'cause they called it by name,
But they'd got a new song to the tune of the same. (2)

Now this was New Dorchester, as they told unto me,
A town very famous in all that country;
They said 'twas new buildings, I grant it is true,
Yet methinks Old Dorchester's as fine as the new. (2)

In Good Old Colony Times

Despite the stern New England puritanical injunctions against singing anything other than psalms, the unaccompanied singing of ballads was a favorite diversion. An "underground" unpublished repertoire of popular songs flourished in the oral tradition. Many of these songs later found their way into 18th-century broadsides.

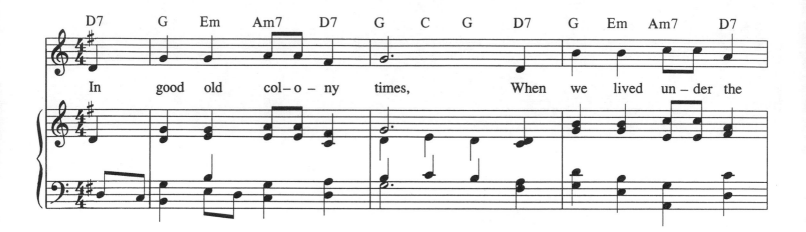

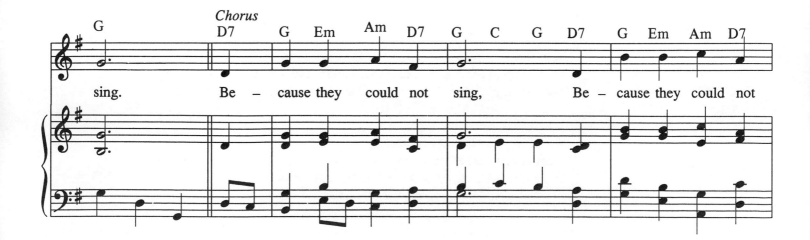

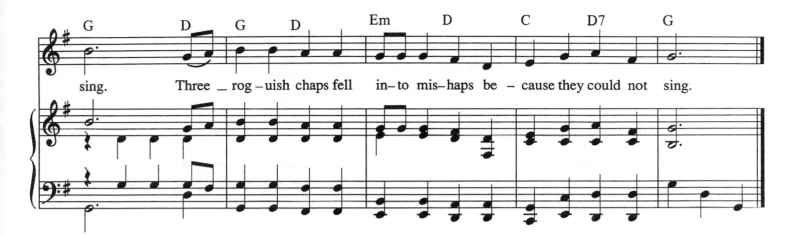

O the first, he was a miller
And the second, he was a weaver,
And the third, he was a little tailor,
Three roguish chaps together.

Chorus: Three roguish chaps together   (2)
        And the third he was a little tailor,
        Three roguish chaps together.

O the miller, he stole corn,
And the weaver, he stole yarn,
And the little tailor ran right away
With the broadcloth under his arm.

Chorus: With the broadcloth under his arm,   (2)
        And the little tailor ran right away
        With the broadcloth under his arm.

The miller was drowned in his dam,
And the weaver got hung in his yarn,
And the Devil clapped his paw on the little tailor
With the broadcloth under his arm.

Chorus: With the broadcloth under his arm,   (2)
        And the devil clapped his paw on the little tailor
        With the broadcloth under his arm.

Courtesy of New York Public Library Picture Collection

The Revolutionary War
1775–1781

Revolutionary Tea

On December 16, 1773, an outraged group of colonists disguised as "Mohawk Indians" dumped 342 chests of English tea into Boston harbor. This famous Boston Tea Party was in response to a tax of threepence a pound levied on all tea imported by the Colonies.

There was an old la–dy lived o–ver the sea, And she was an
old la–dy's pock–ets were filled up with gold; But nev–er con–

Is– land Queen._____ Her__ daugh–ter lived off in a new__ coun–
tent–ed was she._____ So she called on her daugh–ter to pay her a

try, With an o–cean of wa–ter be–tween._____ The tea,
tax of__ three pence a pound on the

Of three pence a pound on the tea._____

"Now, mother, dear mother," the daughter replied.
"I sha'n't do the thing that you ax.
I'm willing to pay a fair price for the tea,
But never a threepenny tax."
  "You shall!" quoth mother, and reddened with rage,
  "For you're my own daughter, you see.
  And sure, 'tis quite proper the daughter should pay
  Her mother a tax on the tea.   (2)

And so the old lady her servant called up,
And packed off a budget of tea.
And eager for three pence a pound, she put in
Enough for a large family.
  She ordered her servant to bring home the tax,
  Declaring her child should obey,
  Or old as she was and a woman most grown,
  She'd half wihip her life away.   (2)

The tea was conveyed to the daughter's door.
All down by the oceanside.
But the bouncing girl poured out every last pound
In the dark and the boiling tide.
  And then she called out to the Island Queen,
  "Oh, mother dear mother," quoth she.
  "Your tea you may have when it is steeped enough,
  But never a tax from me.   (2)

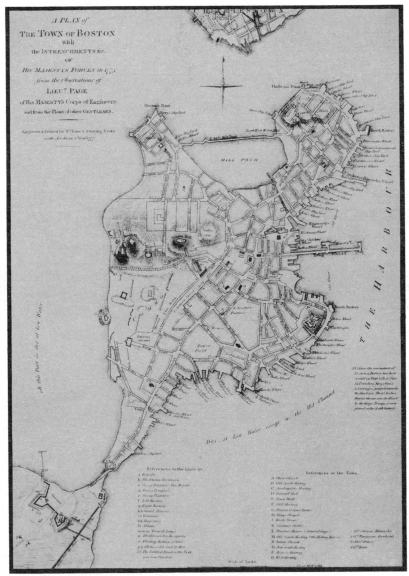

Courtesy of New York Public Library Picture Collection

Free America

Dr. Joseph Warren, who wrote this song in 1774 (borrowing the melody of "The British Grenadiers"), was one of the most prominent of early revolutionary leaders. It was he who dispatched Paul Revere on his famous midnight ride. Warren was killed at the Battle of Bunker Hill at the age of 34 (June 17, 1775).

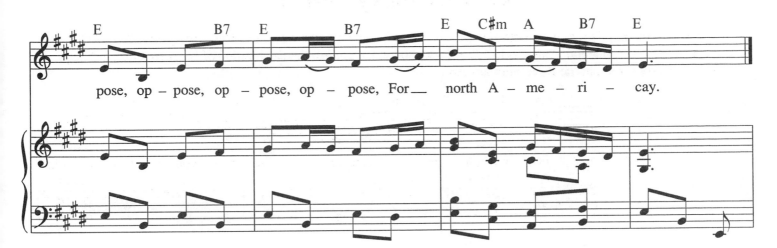

pose, op – pose, op – pose, op – pose, For __ north A – me – ri – cay.

We led fair Freedom hither,
And lo, the desert smiled!
A paradise of pleasure
Was opened in the wild!
Your harvest, bold Americans,
No power shall snatch away!
Huzza, huzza, huzza, huzza,
  For free Americay.

Torn from a world of tyrants,
Beneath this western sky,
We formed a new dominion,
A land of liberty.
The world shall own we're masters here,
Then hasten on the day:
Oppose, oppose, oppose, oppose,
  For free Americay.

Lift up your hands, ye heroes,
And swear with proud disdain,
The wretch that would ensnare you,
Shall lay his snares in vain:
Should Europe empty all her force,
We'll meet her in array,
And fight and shout, and shout and fight
  For North Americay.

Some future day shall crown us
The masters of the main,
Our fleets shall speak in thunder
To England, France and Spain;
And the nations over the ocean spread
Shall tremble and obey
The sons, the sons, the sons, the sons
  Of brave Americay.

Courtesy of New York Public Library Picture Collection 19

The Liberty Song

To the tune of the English song "Hearts of Oak," John Dickinson wrote the words of "The Liberty Song" in 1768. As a delegate to the Continental Congress in 1776, Dickinson voted *against* the Declaration of Independence, although he subsequently served in the Revolutionary Army.

Come join hand in hand, brave A – mer – i – cans all, And rouse your bold hearts at fair

Lib – er – ty's call; No ty – ran – nous acts shall sup – press your just claim, Or

stain with dis-hon – or A – mer – i – ca's name. In free-dom we're born, and in free-dom we'll live, Our

pur-ses are_ read-y, Stead – y, friends, stead-y. Not as slaves,_ but as free-men, our mon-ey we'll give

Our worthy forefathers - let's give them a cheer
To climates unknown did courageously steer;
Through oceans to deserts, for freedom they came,
And dying, bequeathed us their freedom and fame. *Chorus*

Their generous bosoms all dangers despised,
So highly, so wisely, their birthrights they prized;
We'll keep what they gave, we will piously keep,
Nor frustrate their toils on the land or the deep. *Chorus*

The Tree their own hands had to Liberty reared,
They lived to behold growing strong and revered;
With transport they cried, "Now **our wishes we gain**,
For our children shall gather the fruits of our pain." *Chorus*

How sweet are the labors that freemen endure,
That they shall enjoy all the profit, secure
No more such sweet labors Americans know,
If Britons shall reap what Americans sow. *Chorus*

Swarms of placemen and pensioners soon will appear,
Like locusts deforming the charms of the year:
Suns vainly will rise, showers vainly descend,
If we are to drudge for what others shall spend. *Chorus*

Then join hand in hand brave Americans all,
By uniting we stand, by dividing we fall;
In so righteous a cause let us hope to succeed,
For Heaven approves of each generous deed. *Chorus*

All ages shall speak with amaze and applause,
Of the courage we'll show in support of our laws;
To die we can bear - but to serve we disdain,
For shame is to freemen more dreadful than pain. *Chorus*

This bumper I crown for our sovereign's health,
And this for Britannia's glory and wealth;
That wealth and that glory immortal may be,
If she is but just and we are but free. *Chorus*

Capture of Fort Ticonderoga   Courtesy of New York Public Library Picture Collection

Courtesy of New York Public Library Picture Collection

Johnny Has Gone For A Soldier

In the grand tradition of borrowing well-known melodies and fitting new words to them, comes "Johnny Has Gone For A Soldier." It is based on the Irish song "Shule Agrah" ("Come with me, my love"), which dates from the Treaty of Limerick (1691). At that time many Irish patriots fled to France, where they served in the French army in its battles against the British. During the French and Indian War (1756–1763), the Irish adapted the song to sing of the battles of North America in which Irish conscripts in the British army took part. During the Revolutionary War period, Irish immigrants were ardent supporters of the revolutionary cause, as might have been expected, since it gave them an opportunity to fight against the English. And since every Irish man and woman knew "Shule Agrah," the song's metamorphosis into "Johnny Has Gone For A Soldier" was a natural one.

Me, oh my, I loved him so,
Broke my heart to see him go,
And only time will heal my woe,
Johnny has gone for a soldier.

I'll sell my rod, I'll sell my reel,
Likewise I'll sell my spinning wheel,
And buy my love a sword of steel,
Johnny has gone for a soldier.

I'll dye my dress, I'll dye it red,
And through the streets I'll beg for bread,
For the lad that I love from me has fled,
Johnny has gone for a soldier.

Courtesy of New York Public Library Picture Collection

The War of 1812

The Constitution and the Guerrière

On June 18, 1812, at the urging of President James Madison, Congress declared war on Britain. On August 19, the *U.S.S. Constitution,* commanded by Captain Isaac Hull, defeated the British frigate *Guerrière* off the coast of Nova Scotia. It was the first American naval victory of the war.

It off – times has been told That Brit – ish sea – men bold Could flog the tars of France so neat and han – dy – O! But they ner – er found their match, Till the Yan – kees did them catch, O, the Yan – kee boys for fight – ing are the dan – dy O!

The *Guerrière,* a frigate bold,
On the foaming ocean rolled,
Commanded by proud Dacres, the grandee, O!
With as choice a British crew
As a rammer ever drew,
Could flog the Frenchmen two to one so handy, O!

When this frigate hove in view,
Says proud Dacres to his crew,
"Come, clear ship for action and be handy, O!
To the weather gage, boys, get her,"
And to make his men fight better,
Gave them to drink, gunpowder mixed with brandy, O!

Then Dacres loudly cries,
"Make this Yankee ship your prize,
You can in thirty minutes, neat and handy, O!
Twenty-five's enough I'm sure,
And if you'll do it in a score,
I'll treat you to a double share of brandy, O!"

The British shot flew hot,
Which the Yankee answered not,
Till they got within the distance they called handy, O!
"Now," says Hull unto his crew,
"Boys, let's see what we can do,
If we take this boasting Briton, we're the dandy," O!

The first broadside we poured
Carried her mainmast by the board,
Which made this lofty frigate look abandoned, O!
Then Dacres shook his head,
And to his officers, he said,
"Lord! I didn't think those Yankees were so handy, O!"

Our second told so well,
That their fore and mizzen fell,
Which doused the royal ensign neat and handy, O!
"By George." says he, "we're done,"
And they fired a lee gun,
While the Yankees struck up Yankee Doodle Dandy, O!

Then Dacres came on board
To deliver up his sword,
Though loath was he to part with it, 'twas so handy, O!
"O! keep your sword," says Hull,
"For it only makes you dull,
Cheer up and let us have a little brandy, O!"

Now fill your glasses full,
And we'll drink to Captain Hull,
And so merrily we'll push about the brandy, O!
John Bull may toast his fill,
But let the world say what they will,
The Yankee boys for fighting are the dandy, O!

The *Constitution* Capturing His B.M. Frigate *Guerrière*

Ye Parliament of England

With the defeat of Napoleon at Waterloo in 1814, the British were able to turn their full military attentions to their former colonies. But Commodore Oliver Perry's defeat of a British squadron on Lake Erie in September 1813 had imbued the Americans with a great sense of self-confidence. ("Rodgers" refers to Commodore John Rodgers, commander of the frigate *President;* "Decatur" is Stephen Decatur, U.S. naval commander; "Enterprising" refers to the *U.S.S. Enterprise,* which battled the *H.M.S. Boxer* on September 5, 1813, off Portland, Maine.)

Ye Par – lia – ment of Eng – land, Ye Lords and com – mons, too, ____ Con-sid – er well what you're a – bout and what you mean to do. ____ You're now at war with Yan – kees, and I'm sure you'll rue the day ____ You roused the sons of Li – ber – ty in North A – me – ri – cay. ____

You first confined our commerce and said our ships shan't trade,
You next impressed our seamen and used them as your slaves;
You then insulted Rodgers while ploughing o'er the main,
And had we not declared war, you'd have done it o'er again.

You thought our frigates were but few and Yankees could not fight,
Until bold Hull the *Guerrière* took, and banished her from sight.
The *Wasp* then took your *Frolic*, you nothing said to that,
The *Poictiers* being off the coast, of course you took her back.

The next your *Macedonian*, no finer ship could swim,
Decatur took her gilt-work off and then he took her in.
The *Java*, by a Yankee ship was sunk, you all must know,
The *Peacock* fine, in all her prime, by Lawrence down did go.

Then next you sent your *Boxer* to box us all about,
But we had an Enterprising brig that beat your *Boxer* out;
We boxed her up to Portland and moored her off the town
To show the sons of liberty this *Boxer* of renown.

Then next upon Lake Erie, brave Perry had some fun;
You own he beat your naval force and caused them for to run;
This was to you a sore defeat, the like ne'er known before,
Your British squadron beat complete, some took, some run ashore.

Then your brave Indian allies, you styled them that by name,
Until they turned their tomahawks, and by you, savages became.
Your mean insinuations they despised from their souls,
And joined the sons of liberty that scorn to be controlled.

There's Rodgers in the *President*, will burn, sink and destroy;
The *Congress*, on the Brazil coast, your commerce will annoy;
The *Essex*, in the South Seas, will put out all your lights,
The flag she waves at her mast-head: "Free Trade and Sailor's Rights."

Lament, ye sons of Britain, far distant is the day
That e'er you'll gain what you have lost in North Americay.
Go tell your king and Parliament, by all the world it's known,
That British force, by sea and land's by Yankees overthrown.

Use every endeavor, and strive to make a peace,
For Yankee ships are building fast, their navy to increase;
They will enforce their commerce, the laws by heaven are made,
That Yankee ships, in time of peace, to any port may trade.

Grant us free trade and commerce and don't impress our men,
Give up all claims of Canada, then we'll be at peace again;
And then we will respect you and treat you as our friend,
Respect our flag and citizens, then all these wars will end.

1815 etching by Wm. Charles. "John Bull Before New Orleans"
John Bull between an American rifleman & a Franco–American supporter

The Patriotic Diggers

The British capture and burning of Washington on August 24, 1814, created panic all along the Atlantic coast. Although the British never attacked New York ("Brooklyn Heights"), their bombardment of Fort McHenry in Chesapeake Bay inspired the writing of "The Star-Spangled Banner" by Francis Scott Key.

By Samuel Woodworth

John–ny Bull, be–ware! Keep your prop–er dis–tance, Else we'll make you stare

at our firm re–sis–tance. Let a–lone the lads Who are free–dom tast–ing

Re–col–lect our dads gave you once a bast–ing. Pick-axe, shov–el, spade,

crow-bar, hoe and bar-row, Bet-ter not in – vade, Yank-ees have the mar-row.

To protect our rights, 'gainst your flints and triggers,
See on Brooklyn Heights, our patriotic diggers.
Men of every age, color, rank, profession,
Ardently engage, labor in succession. *Chorus*

Grandeur leaves her towers, poverty her hovel,
Here to join their powers with the hoe and shovel,
Here the merchant toils with the patriotic sawyer
There the laborer smiles, near him sweats the lawyer. *Chorus*

Here the mason builds freedom's shrine of glory,
While the painter gilds the immortal story;
Blacksmiths catch the flame, grocers feel the spirit
Printers share the fame and record their merit. *Chorus*

Scholars leave their schools with their patriotic teachers,
Farmers seize their tools, headed by their preachers,
How they break the soil - brewers, butchers, bakers
Here the doctors toil, there the undertakers. *Chorus*

Bright Apollo's sons leave their pipe and tabor,
Mid the roar of guns, join the martial labor.
Round th'embattled plain in sweet concord rally,
And in freedom's strain, sing the foe's finale. *Chorus*

Plumbers, founders, dyers, tinmen, turners, shavers,
Sweepers, clerks and criers, jewelers, engravers,
Clothiers, drapers, players, cartmen, hatters, tailors,
Gaugers, sealers, weighers, carpenters and sailors. *Chorus*

Better not invade, recollect the spirit,
Which our dads displayed and their sons inherit;
If you still advance,friendly caution slighting,
You may get by chance a belly-full of fighting. *Chorus*

The Battle of New Orleans

On January 8, 1815, the American forces under Andrew Jackson defeated the British under Sir Edward Packenham in the last engagement of the War of 1812. The battle of New Orleans was a great vicory. Unfortunately, it was fought two weeks after the signing of the peace treaty between the Americans and the British at Ghent.

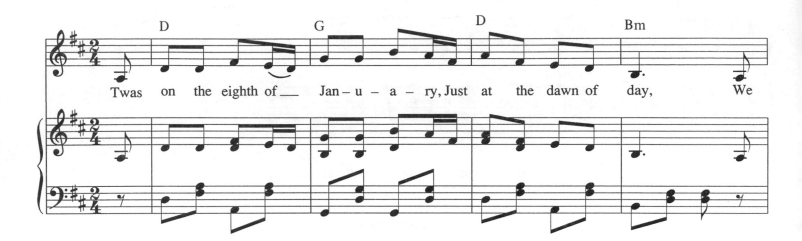

Twas on the eighth of ___ Jan – u – a – ry, Just at the dawn of day, We

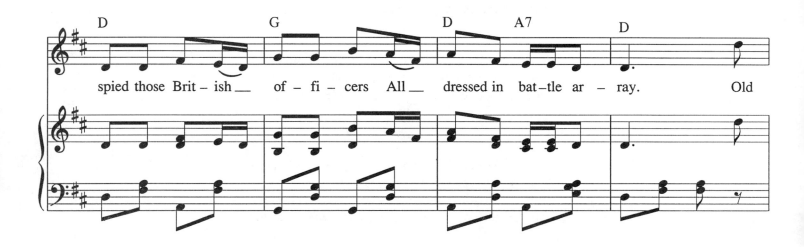

spied those Brit – ish ___ of – fi – cers All ___ dressed in bat – tle ar – ray. Old

Jack – son then gave ___ or – ders, "Each man to keep his post, And

form a line from _ right to left, And _ let no time be lost."

With rockets and with bombshells, like comets we let fly;
Like lions they advanced us, the fate of war to try;
Large streams of fiery vengeance upon them we let pour,
While many a brave commander lay withering in his gore.

Thrice they marched up to the charge, and thrice they gave the ground;
We fought them full three hours, then bugle horns did sound.
Great heaps of human pyramids lay strewn before our eyes;
We blew the horns and rang the bells to drown their dying cries.

Come all you British noblemen and listen unto me;
Our Frontiersman has proved to you America is free.
But tell your royal master when you return back home,
That out of thirty thousand men, but few of you returned.

Courtesy of New York Public Library Picture Collection

Courtesy of New York Public Library Picture Collection

Texas and Mexico 1836–1848

Courtesy of New York Public Library Picture Collection

Remember The Alamo

On February 23, 1836, the Mexican army under Santa Ana — some 3,000 strong — lay siege to a garrison of 1,871 Texans in an old Spanish mission in San Antonio: the Alamo. It took the attacking Mexicans almost two weeks to breach the walls of the Alamo. They had orders to kill every Texan. When they finally overcame the defenders on March 6, among the dead were frontier heroes Davy Crockett and Jim Bowie. Six weeks later, Sam Houston addressed his troops before the fateful battle of San Jacinto: "The army will cross and we will meet the enemy. Some of us may be killed, must be killed: but, soldiers, remember the Alamo! The Alamo! The Alamo!"

Words by T.A. Durriage
Music: Bruce's Address

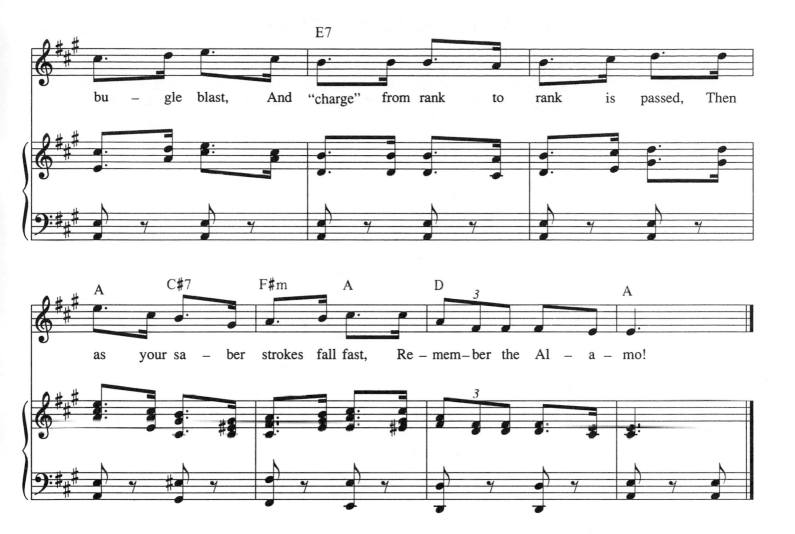

bu — gle blast, And "charge" from rank to rank is passed, Then

as your sa — ber strokes fall fast, Re — mem — ber the Al — a — mo!

Heed not the Spanish battle yell,
Let every stroke we give them tell,
And let them fall as Crockett fell.
    Remember the Alamo!

For every wound and every thrust
On prisoners dealt by hands accurst,
A Mexican shall bite the dust.
    Remember the Alamo!

The cannon's peal shall ring their knell,
Each volley sound a passing bell,
Each cheer Columbia's vengeance tell.
    Remember the Alamo!

For if, disdaining flight, they stand
And try the issue hand to hand.
Woe to each Mexican brigand!
    Remember the Alamo!

Sung to last 8 measures.
Then boot and saddle! Draw the sword!
Unfurl your banners bright and broad,
And as ye smite the murderous horde,
    Remember the Alamo!

The Song of Texas

By 1846, the United States had decided that its logical western border should run from San Diego to the Pacific and up to Oregon. General Zachary Taylor led the American forces to keep the Mexicans from crossing the Rio Grande. His victories led to the annexation of Texas as well as the acquisition of California, Nevada and Utah, most of Arizona and New Mexico and parts of Wyoming and Colorado.

I fear no haugh–ty na–tion, Though foes all 'round are piled, For

now I take my sta–tion as ___ Un – cle Sam – my's child.

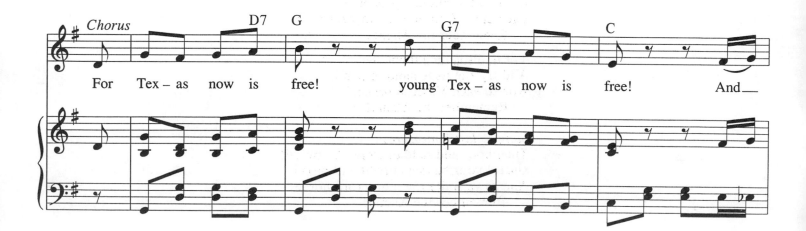

Chorus
For Tex – as now is free! young Tex – as now is free! And ___

When I shine a – mong the stars, How hap – py I shall be!

Though Mexico in pride now,
Begins to threaten blows,
I'll grin at Sammy's side now,
With my thumb upon my nose. *Chorus*

In 'thirty-six I was of age,
Took Liberty's degrees,
And to unite I have a right,
With any state I please. *Chorus*

In Liberty's pure laws, now,
Uncle Sam and I are one,
And I will aid his cause, now,
For Sister Oregon. *Chorus*

With Freedom's fire prolific,
We'll clear our rightful bound,
From Atlantic to Pacific
Is Uncle Sam's own ground.

Last Chorus
The whole shall yet be free,
The whole shall yet be free,
And Uncle Sam shall have it all
In peace and Liberty.

Green Grow The Lilacs

This is yet another borrowing from an old Irish folk song ("Green Grows the Laurel"). In that song it is the woman who complains about her faithless lover. The American version proved so popular with the troops fighting against the Mexicans that, it has been said, the pejorative term *gringo* (from "green grows") comes from the Mexican mis-hearing of the words. Whether that story is true or not is impossible to say. What we do know is that an Oklahoman poet named Lynn Riggs wrote a play using the song's title. That play subsequently was adapted into the musical *Oklahoma!*

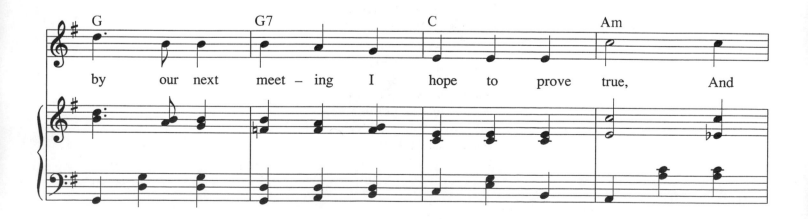

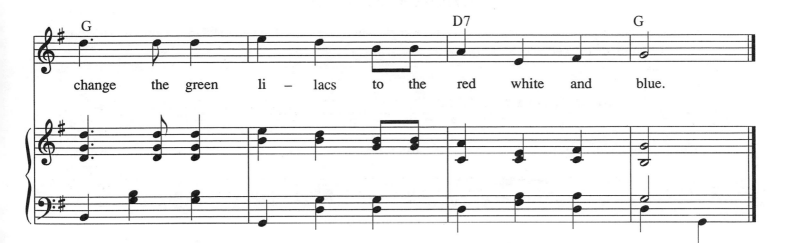

change the green li – lacs to the red white and blue.

I used to have a sweetheart, but now I have none
Since she's gone and left me, I care not for one.
Since she's gone and left me, contented I'll be,
For she loves another one better than me.

I passed my love's window, both early and late,
The look that she gave me, it made my heart ache.
Oh, the look that she gave me was painful to see,
For she loves another one better than me.

I wrote my love letters in rosy red lines,
She sent me an answer all twisted in twines,
Saying, "Keep your love letter and don't waste your time,
Just you write to your love and I'll write to mine.

Repeat first verse

Santy Anno

In the years following the Mexican War, songs concerning the defeated Mexican general Santa Ana began to appear in American and British sea chanteys.

Chorus
So heave her up and away we'll go.
Heave away, Santy Anno;
Heave her up and away we'll go.
All on the plains of Mexico.

She's a fast clipper ship and a bully
  good crew,
Heave away, Santy Anno.
A down-East Yankee for her captain,
  too.
All on the plains of Mexico. *Chorus*

There's plenty of gold so I've been told,
Heave away, Santy Anno.
There's plenty of gold so I've been told,
Way out west to Californi-o. *Chorus*

Back in the days of Forty-nine,
Heave away, Santy Anno.
Those are the days of the good old
  times,
All on the plains of Mexico. *Chorus*

When Zachary Taylor gained the
  day,
Heave away, Santy Anno.
He made poor Santy run away,
All on the plains of Mexico. *Chorus*

General Scott and Taylor, too,
Heave away, Santy Anno.
Made poor Santy meet his Waterloo,
All on the plains of Mexico. *Chorus*

When I leave the ship, I will settle
  down,
Heave away, Santy Anno.
And marry a girl named Sally Brown,
All on the plains of Mexico. *Chorus*

Santy Anno was a good old man,
Heave away, Santy Anno.
'Til he got into war with your Uncle
  Sam,
All on the plains of Mexico. *Chorus*

42

The Gold Rush
1849–1850s

Banks of the Sacramento

In 1849 there were two ways to get from the east coast to the gold fields of California: Overland by covered wagon across the Great Plains, the desert and the high Sierras or by water around Cape Horn. Either way you might make it - or you might not. Then the clipper ship was born. In 1851, the swiftest afloat was the *Flying Cloud* - New York to San Francisco in 89 days and 20 hours. That was something to sing about!.

Words: Traditional
Music: Stephen Foster, Camptown Races

In the Black Ball Line I served my time, with a hoo-dah, with a hoo-dah; In a full-rigged ship and in her prime, with a hoo-dah, - hoo-dah day.

Chorus

So blow, blow,— blow for Cal-i-for-ni-O. There's plen-ty of gold, so I've been told, On the banks of the Sac-ra - men-to.

O we were the boys to make her go. . .
Around Cape Horn in the frost and snow . . . *Chorus*

Around Cape Stiff in seventy days . . .
Around Cape Stiff is a mighty long ways . . . *Chorus*

When we was tacking 'round Cape Horn . . .
I often wished I'd a never been born. . . *Chorus*

O the mate he whacked me around and around . . .
And I wished I was home all safe and sound. . . *Chorus*

O when we got to the Frisco docks . . .
The girls all were in their Sunday frocks . . . *Chorus*

Molly Durkin

The discovery of gold in California in 1848 coincided with the great potato famine in Ireland. In the following years a great wave of Irish immigration washed upon our shores. Here, the broken-hearted young man makes his fortune in "Califoony" and returns to Ireland.

I'm a da–cint hon-est work-in' man, as you might un—der–stand, And I'll tell to you the rea—son why I left old I–re–land. 'Twas Mol–ly Dur-kin did it when she mar-ried Tim O'–shea, And to keep my heart from

Well, I landed in Castle Garden,* sure I met a man named Burke
And he told me remain in New York until he got me work.
But he hasn't got it for me, so tonight I'll tell him plain,
For San Francisco in the morn I'm going to take a train. *Chorus*

Well, I'm out in Cal-i-forn-i and my fortune it is made.
I'm a-loaded down with gold and I throw away my pick and spade,
Sail home to dear old Ireland with the Castle out of sight,
And I'll marry Miss O'Kelly, Molly Durkin for to spite. *Chorus*

*Castle Garden was the immigrant reception center in New York before Ellis Island was used.

47

California

This is my translation of a Danish immigrant song which was written by Erik Bogh in 1850. It was published in Copenhagen by Julius Strandberg, who specialized in popular literature and street ballads. Songs about America were extremely popular in 19th-century Denmark.

And there all beggars lead happy lives,
  Without worry.
And when they marry, take many wives,
  There's no hurry.
There one can live as it pleases you,
  Without risk-o.
Were I a girl I would travel to
  San Francisco.

Yes, every man has a slave today,
  It's quite funny.
And even children are used to play
  With real money.
And if a fellow decides to save,
  He's demented.
Why, you can have everything you crave ——
  Be contented.

And there a poor man's a millionaire,
  Yes indeedy!
And even Rothschild cannot compare
  He'd be needy.
It is a land where you pay your tax
  To financemen.
And so I'm off - may you all relax,
  My dear landsmen.

The Days of 49

By 1872, when this song was published in San Francisco in *The Great Emerson New Popular Songster*, the Gold Rush was long over. The oldtimers would sit around and swap tall tales and tell each other stories (some of them true) of what they had done in the days of "forty-nine."

I'm old Tom Moore from the bum-mer's shore, In the good old gold-en
call me a bum-mer and a gin sot too, But what cares I for

days. They praise? I wan-der a-round from town-to town, Just

like a rov-ing sign; And the peo-ple all say, "There goes Tom Moore, of the

Chorus

days of for – ty – nine." In the days of old, in the days of gold, How oft–times I re –
pine For the days of old, when we dug up the gold in the days of for – ty – nine.

My comrades they all loved me well,
A jolly, saucy crew,
A few hard cases I will admit,
Though they were brave and true;
Whatever the pinch, they ne'er would flinch,
They never would fret or whine,
Like good old bricks, they stood the kicks
In the days of forty-nine. *Chorus*

There was old Lame Jess, a hard old cuss,
Who never did repent;
He never was known to miss a drink
Or ever spend a cent;
But old Lame Jess, like all the rest,
To death he did resign,
And in his bloom went up the flume
In the days of forty-nine. *Chorus*

There was Poker Bill, one of the boys,
Who was always in for a game,
Whether he lost or whether he won,
To him it was all the same;
He would ante up and draw his cards
He would go you a hatful blind,
In the game with death Bill lost his breath
In the days of forty-nine. *Chorus*

There was New York Jake, the butcher's boy,
He was always getting tight,
And every time that he'd get full
He was spoiling for a fight;
Then Jake rampaged against a knife
In the hands of old Bob Sine;
And over Jake they held a wake
In the days of forty-nine. *Chorus*

There was Ragshag Bill from Buffalo
I never will forget,
He would roar all day and roar all night,
And I guess he's roaring yet;
One night he fell in a prospect hole
In a roaring bad design;
And in that hole he roared out his soul
In the days of forty-nine. *Chorus*

Of all the comrades that I've had
There's none that's left to boast;
And I'm left alone in my misery
Like some poor wandering ghost;
And as I pass from town to town
They call me the rambling sign,
"There goes Tom Moore, a bummer shore,
Of the days of forty-nine." *Chorus*

51

Courtesy of New York Public Library Picture Collection

Settling the West 1850–1875

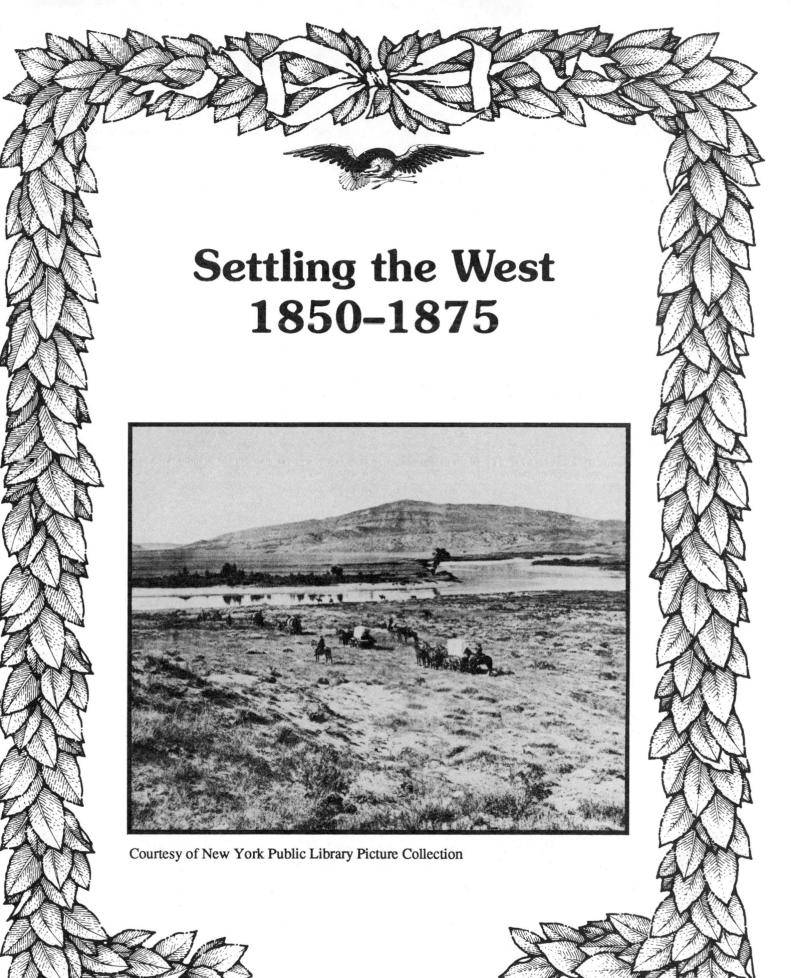

Courtesy of New York Public Library Picture Collection

The Homestead of the Free

Subtitled "Song of the Kansas Emigrant," this song grew out of the Kansas–Nebraska Act of 1854. The Act established the principle of "popular sovereignty" concerning slavery. The people of these territories would decide for themselves before applying for admission to the Union whether slavery would be legal in their states. In 1855, the New England Emigrant Aid Committee was organized to encourage the settlement of anti-slavery families in Kansas. The New England poet John Greenleaf Whittier wrote the words to this song in 1854 upon the departure of a party of settlers for the Kansas plains.

Words by John Greenleaf Whittier

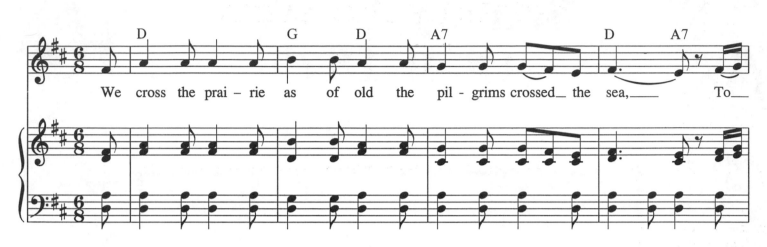

We cross the prai – rie as of old the pil - grims crossed the sea, To

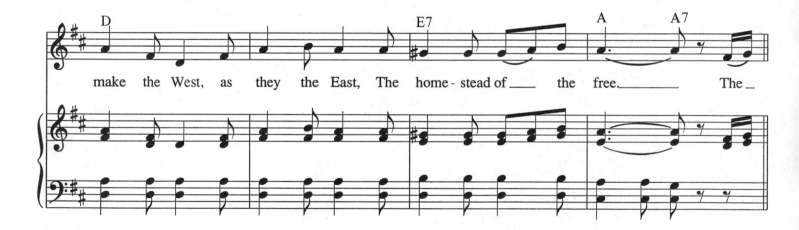

make the West, as they the East, The home - stead of the free. The

home – stead of the free, my boys, The home – stead of the free. To

make the West, as they the East, The__ home – stead of the free._____

We go to rear a wall of men
On freedom's southern line,
And plant beside the cotton bale
The rugged northern pine. *Chorus*

We go to plant her common schools
On distant prairie swells;
And give the sabbath of the wild
The music of her bells. *Chorus*

Up-bearing, like the ark of old,
The Bible in our van;
We go to test the truth of God
Against the fraud of man. *Chorus*

Sweet Betsy from Pike

John A. Stone was a one-time gold prospector in the California gold fields in the 1850s. Assuming the name "Old Put," he became San Francisco's foremost minstrel composer and singing voice of the Gold Rush. In 1858 he published *Put's Golden Songster,* in which this song, his own composition, appeared. The melody is the British music-hall song "Villikins and His Dinah."

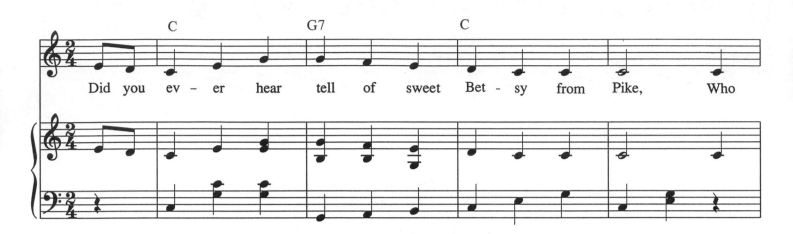

Did you ev – er hear tell of sweet Bet – sy from Pike, Who

crossed the wide prai – ries with her lov – er, Ike; With two yoke of

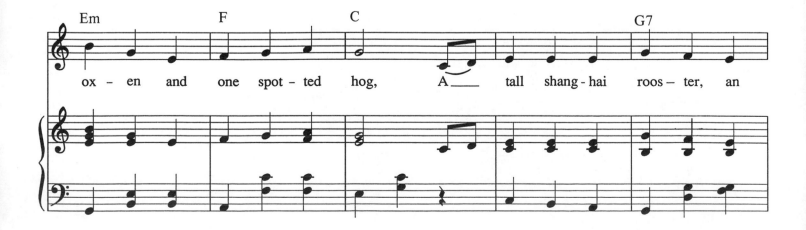

ox – en and one spot – ted hog, A___ tall shang – hai roos – ter, an

old yel - low dog? Sing ___ too - ral - i, oo - ral - i oo - ral - i - ay.

One evening quite early they camped on the Platte,
'Twas near by the road on a green shady flat;
Where Betsy, quite tired, lay down to repose,
While with wonder Ike gazed on his Pike County rose.
Chorus

Out on the prairie one bright starry night
They broke out the whisky and Betsy got tight.
She sang and she shouted and danced o'er the plain,
And showed her bare arse to the whole wagon train.
Chorus

They stopped at Salt Lake to inquire the way,
Where Brigham declared that sweet Betsy should stay.
But Betsy got frightened and ran like a deer,
While Brigham stood pawing the ground like a steer.
Chorus

The Injuns came down in a wild yelling horde,
And Betsy was skeered they would scalp her adored.
Behind the front wagon wheel Betsy did crawl,
And fought off the Injuns with musket and ball.
Chorus

They soon reached the desert where Betsy gave out,
And down in the sand she lay rolling about.
While Ike in great terror looked on in surprise,
Saying, "Betsy, get up, you'll get sand in your eyes."
Chorus

The alkali desert was burning and bare,
And Isaac's soul shrank from the death that lurked there:
"Dear old Pike County, I'll go back to you."
Says Betsy, "You'll go by yourself if you do."
Chorus

The Shanghai ran off and their cattle all died.
That morning the last piece of bacon was fried.
Poor Ike got discouraged and Betsy got mad,
The dog drooped his tail and looked wondrously sad.
Chorus

They swam the wide rivers and crossed the tall peaks,
They camped on the prairie for weeks upon weeks.
Starvation and cholera, hard work and slaughter,
They reached California spite of hell and high water.
Chorus

One morning they climbed up a very high hill,
And with wonder looked down upon old Placerville.
Ike shouted and said, as he cast his eyes down,
"Sweet Betsy, my darling, we're got to Hangtown."
Chorus

Long Ike and sweet Betsy attended a dance,
And Ike wore a pair of his Pike County pants.
Sweet Betsy was dressed up in ribbons and rings,
Says Ike, "You're an angel, but where are your wings?"
Chorus

A miner said, "Betsy, will you dance with me?"
"I will, you old hoss, if you don't make too free.
But don't dance me hard — do you want to know why?
Doggone ye, I'm chock-full of strong alkali!"
Chorus

Long Ike and sweet Betsy got married, of course,
But Ike, getting jealous, obtained a divorce.
And Betsy, well satisfied, said with a shout,
"Good-bye, you big lummox, I'm glad you backed out!"
Chorus

Acres of Clams

Hard luck, more often than not, was the fate of the gold seeker. But other wonders of the West opened up for those willing and able to move on. The tune to this song is the Irish "Old Rosin, the Beau."

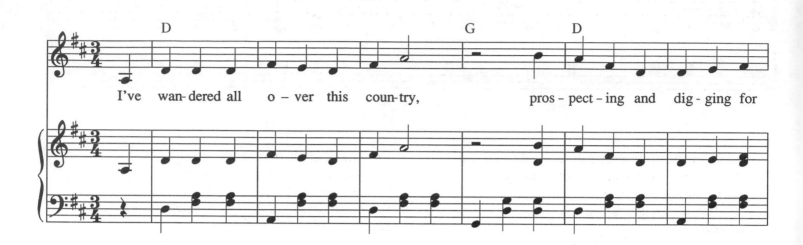

I've wan-dered all o – ver this coun-try, pros – pect – ing and dig - ging for

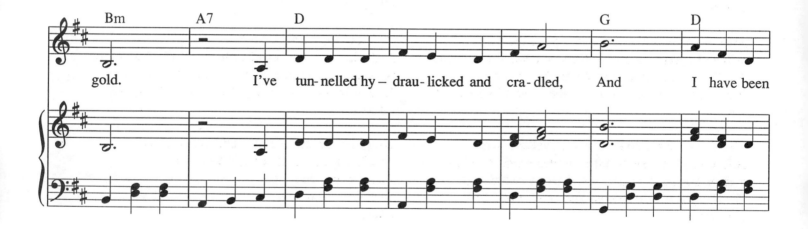

gold. I've tun-nelled hy – drau-licked and cra-dled, And I have been

fre-quent-ly sold, And I have been fre-quent-ly sold,

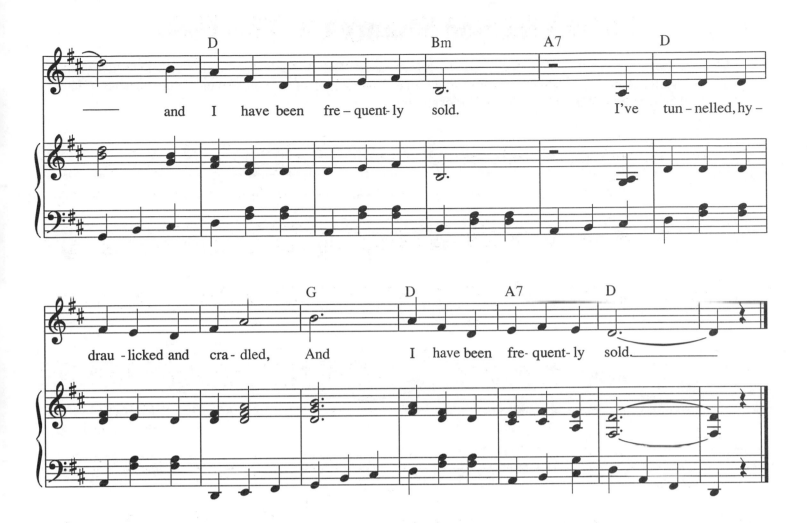

and I have been fre–quent-ly sold. I've tun–nelled, hy–drau-licked and cra-dled, And I have been fre-quent-ly sold.

For one who gets riches by mining,
Perceiving that hundreds grow poor,
I made up my mind to try farming,
The only pursuit that is sure.

Chorus: The only pursuit that is sure, (2)
I made up my mind to try farming,
The only pursuit that is sure.

So, rolling my grub in a blanket,
I left all my tools on the ground.
And I started one morning to shank it
For the country they call Puget Sound.

Chorus For the country . . .

Arriving flat broke in midwinter,
The ground was enveloped in fog;
And covered all over with timber
Thick as hair on the back of a dog.

Chorus: Thick as hair . . .

When I looked at the prospects so gloomy
The tears trickled over my face;
And I thought that my travels had brought me
To the end of the jumping-off place.

Chorus: To the end . . .

I staked me a claim in the forest
And set myself down to hard toil.
For two years I chopped and I struggled,
But I never got down to the soil.

Chorus: But I never . . .

I tried to get out of the country,
But poverty forced me to stay,
Until I became an old settler,
Then nothing could drive me away.

Chorus: Then nothing . . .

And now that I'm used to the country,
I think that if man ever found
A place to live easy and happy,
That Eden is on Puget Sound.

Chorus: That Eden . . .

No longer the slave of ambition,
I laugh at the world and its shams;
As I think of my happy condition,
Surrounded by acres of clams.

Chorus: Surrounded by acres . . .

Little Old Sod Shanty On The Plain

"I've got a little bet with the government," said the homesteader. "They're betting me I can't live here for five years, and I'm betting them I can." Under the terms of the Homestead Act of 1862, a man could claim 160 acres of land provided he worked and lived on his claim for five years.

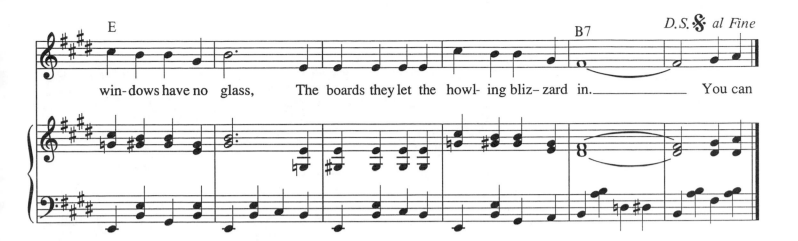

D.S. 𝄋 al Fine

win-dows have no glass, The boards they let the howl- ing bliz- zard in._____ You can

I rather like the novelty of living in this way,
Though my bill of fare isn't always of the best,
But I'm happy as a clam on the land of Uncle Sam,
In my little old sod shanty in the West. *Chorus*

But when I left my Eastern home, a bachelor so gay,
To try and win my way to wealth and fame,
I little thought I'd come down to burning twisted hay
In the little old sod shanty on my claim. *Chorus*

My clothes are plastered o'er with dough, I'm looking like a fright,
And everyting is scattered round the room;
But I wouldn't give the freedom that I have out in the West,
For the table of the Eastern man's old home. *Chorus*

Still, I wish that some kind-hearted girl would pity on me take,
And relieve me from the mess that I am in;
The angel, how I'd bless her if this her home she'd make
In the little old sod shanty on my claim! *Chorus*

And if fate should bless us with now and then an heir
To cheer our hearts with honest pride of fame,
Oh, then we'd be contented for the toil that we had spent
In the little old sod shanty on our claim. *Chorus*

When time enough had lapsed and all those little brats
To noble man and womanhood had grown,
It wouldn't seem half so lonely as round us we should look,
And we'd see the old sod shanty on our claim. *Chorus*

Courtesy of New York Public Library Picture Collection

The Cowboy
1870–1890

The Old Chisholm Trail

Jesse Chisholm (1805-1868) carved out a two hundred and twenty mile trail through the Oklahoma Indian Territory.
He used it to get from his ranch to a trading post on the north fork of the Canadian River.   In the days of the great
cattle drives, the cowboys drove their long-horns over the trail.   It was lengthened from southern Texas all the way
to the railroad in Abilene, Kansas.   It reached its peak of use in 1875 as hundreds of spurs from ranches all over
Texas fed into it.

Well,   come a - long, boys, and   lis – ten to my tale,   And I'll

tell you of my trou - bles on the   old Chis - holm Trail. Come a ti - yi   yip - pee, yip - pee

yay,   yip - pee yay, Come a ti - yi   yip - pee, yip - pee yay.

I started up the trail October twenty-third,
I started up the trail with the 2-U herd. *Chorus*

On a ten-dollar hoss and a forty-dollar saddle,
I'm a-going to punch them Texas cattle. *Chorus*

I jumped in the saddle and grabbed a-holt the horn,
Best durn cowboy ever was born. *Chorus*

I'm up in he morning before daylight,
And before I sleep, the moon shines bright. *Chorus*

It's bacon and beans 'most every day,
I'd as soon been a-eating prairie hay. *Chorus*

Cloudy in the east and it looks like rain,
And my darned old slicker's in the wagon again. *Chorus*

Wind began to blow—rain began to fall,
It looked, by grab, like we was gonna lose 'em all *Chorus*

I went to the boss to draw my roll.
He had me figgered out nine dollars in the hole. *Chorus*

So me and the boss, we had a little chat.
I hit him in the face with my big slouch hat. *Chorus*

So the boss said to me, "I'm gonna fire you—
"And not only you but the whole durn crew." *Chorus*

Well, I'm going back home to draw my money,
Going back home to see my honey. *Chorus*

Well, my feet are in the stirrup and my saddle's in the sky,
And I'll quit punching cows in the Sweet Bye and Bye. *Chorus*

Git Along, Little Dogies

The cowboys said that a dogie is a little calf who has lost its mammy and his daddy's run away with another cow.

As I was a-walk-in' one morn-ing for pleas-ure, I spied a cow-punch-er a-stroll-in' a-long. His hat was thrown back and his spurs were a jing-lin', And as he ap-proached he was sing-ing this

It's early in the spring that we round up the dogies,
We mark them and brand them and bob off their tails;
We round up the horses, load up the chuck wagon,
And then throw the dogies upon the long trail. *Chorus*

Your mother was raised away down in Texas,
Where the jimpson weed and the sand-burrs grow,
Now we'll fill you up on prickly pear and cactus,
Till you are all ready for the trail to Idaho. *Chorus*

Oh, you'll be soup for Uncle Sam's soldiers,
It's "Beef, more beef," I hear them cry.
Git along, git along, git along little dogies,
You'll be beef steers by and by. *Chorus*

I Ride An Old Paint

A paint is a horse with irregular patterns of white and colored areas. The "fiery and snuffy" are spirited or wild cattle. To "throw the houlihan" after roping an animal, the cowboy's horse stops abruptly, causing the roped animal to be thrown to the ground. A coulee is a dry creek, and a draw is a shallow drain that catches rainfall.

backs are all raw. Ride a - round, lit - tle do - gies, Ride a - round____ them____

slow, For the fier - y and snuf - fy are rar - in' to go.

Old Bill Jones had two daughters and a song,
One went to college the other went wrong.
His wife got killed in a pool-room fight,
But still he keeps singing from morning till night. *Chorus*

I've worked in the city, worked on the farm,
And all I've got to show is the muscle in my arm.
Patches on my pants, callous on my hand
And I'm goin' to Montana to throw the houlihan. *Chorus*

When I die, don't bury me at all,
Put me on my pony and lead him from his stall.
Tie my bones to his back, turn our faces to the west,
And we'll ride the prairie that we love the best. *Chorus*

The Tenderfoot

The perennial butt of cowboy humor and practical joking was the innocent tenderfoot or greenhorn.

I thought one day that just for fun I'd see how cow-

punch-ing was done, So when the round-ups had be-gun, I

tack-led a cat-tle king. Says he, "My fore-man's

gone to town. He's at the Red Eye, his name is Brown. If

you see him he'll take you down." Says I, "That's just the thing."____

We started for the ranch next day,
Brown augured me most all the way.
He said that punching was only play,
That it was no work at all;
That all you had to do was ride,
'Twas only drifting with the tide.
The son of a gun, oh how he lied —
He certainly had his gall.

They saddled me up an old gray hack,
With two set fasts on his back,
They padded him down with a gunny sack,
And used by bedding all.
When I got on he left the ground,
Went up in the air and looked around.
While I came down and busted the ground,
And got one hell of a fall.

Sometimes my horse would buck and break
Across the prairie he would take,
As if running for a stake —
It seemed to them but play.
Sometimes I couldn't catch them at all.
Sometimes my horse would slip and fall,
And I'd shoot on like a cannon ball,
'Til the earth came up my way.

They picked me up and carried me in,
And rubbed me down with an old stake-pin.
"That's the way they all begin,
You're doing swell," says Brown.
"And by the morning if you don't die,
I'll give you another horse to try."
"Oh say, can't I walk," says I.
Says he, "Yep, back to town."

I've traveled up, I've traveled down,
I've traveled this country 'round and 'round;
I've lived in city, I've lived in town,
And I've got this much to say:
Before you try cowpunching, kiss your wife,
Take heavy insurance on your life,
Then cut your throat with a carving knife,
It's easier to die that way.

Artist — Thos. Eakins   Courtesy of New York Public Library Picture Collection

Negro Spirituals

Artist — T.W. Wood, 1861   Courtesy of New York Public Library Picture Collection

Go Down, Moses

The great Negro woman Abolitionist leader and ex-slave, Harriet Tubman, may have been the Moses of this song. As a tireless Underground Railroad conductor, she made scores of journeys into slavery's "Egypt land," returning to the North each trip with a band of runaway slaves.

Tell ol' Phar-aoh, To let my peo-ple go.

Thus saith the Lord, bold Moses said,
Let my people go,
If not, I'll smite your first-born dead,
Let my people go. *Chorus*

No more shall they in bondage toil,
Let them come out with Egypt's spoil. *Chorus*

The Lord told Moses what to do,
To lead the Hebrew children through. *Chorus*

O come along Moses, you'll not get lost,
Stretch out your rod and come across. *Chorus*

As Israel stood by the waterside,
At God's command it did divide. *Chorus*

When they reached the other shore,
They sang a song of triumph o'er. *Chorus*

Pharaoh said he'd go across,
But Pharaoh and his host were lost. *Chorus*

Jordan shall stand up like a wall,
And the walls of Jericho shall fall. *Chorus*

Your foes shall not before you stand,
And you'll possess fair Canaan's Land. *Chorus*

O let us all from bondage flee,
And let us all in Christ be free. *Chorus*

We need not always weep and mourn,
And wear these slavery chains forlorn. *Chorus*

Steal Away

"Steal Away" was one of the widest used "signal songs" when slaves wanted to hold a secret conclave somewhere off in the woods. The words abound in imagery which can be interpreted as references to secret meeting places.

trum-pet sounds with-in-a my soul, I ain't got long to stay here.

Green trees are bending,
Poor sinner stands a-trembling;
The trumpet sounds within-a my soul,
I ain't got long to stay here.   *Chorus*

Tombstones are bursting
Poor sinner stands a-trembling;
The trumpet sounds within-a my soul,
I ain't got long to stay here.   *Chorus*

My Lord calls me,
He calls me by the lightning;
The trumpet sounds within-a my soul,
I ain't got long to stay here.   *Chorus*

Wade in the Water

Crossing the Jordan River into the Promised Land is yet another symbol for flight to freedom.

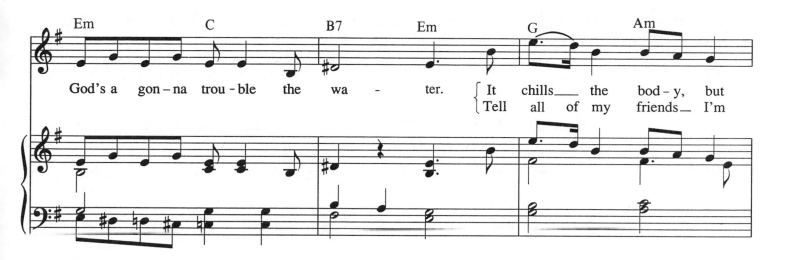

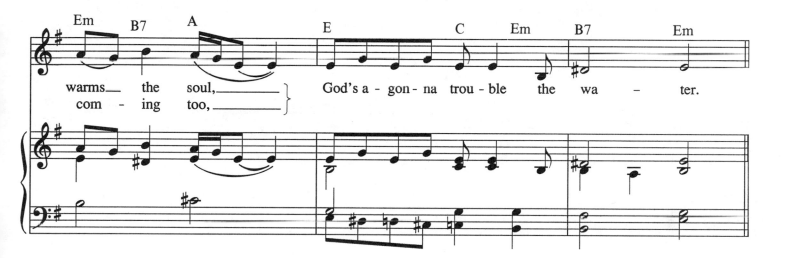

79

Slavery Chain Done Broke At Last

With the Emancipation Proclamation and the end of the Civil War, the old spiritual "Joshua Fit the Battle of Jericho" was transformed into a jubilant hymn of deliverance.

Words: anonymous
Music: Joshua Fit the Battle of Jericho

Slav - e - ry chain___ done___ broke at last,___

Broke at last,___ Broke at last,_____ Slav - e - ry chain - done -

broke at last,___ Gon - na praise God till I die.

Way up in that val - ley, Pray - in' on my knees,

Tell - in' God a - bout my trou - bles, And to help me if He please.

D.C. al Fine

I did tell him how I suffer,
In the dungeon and the chain;
And the days I went with head bowed down,
An' my broken flesh and pain. *Chorus*

I did know my Jesus heard me,
'Cause the spirit spoke to me,
An' said, "Rise my chile, your children,
An' you too shall be free." *Chorus*

I done p'int one mighty captain
For to marshal all my hosts;
An' to bring my bleeding ones to me,
An' not one shall be lost. *Chorus*

Now no more weary trav'lin',
'Cause my Jesus set me free,
An' there's no more auction block for me,
Since He gave me liberty. *Chorus*

81

Anti-Abolitionists attacking printing plant of Abolitionist editor Elijah P. Lovejoy in Alton, Ill., Nov. 1837.
Courtesy of New York Public Library Picture Collection

Abolition 1840–1861

—VOL. I. NO. 5.—

THE
AMERICAN
ANTI-SLAVERY
ALMANAC,
FOR

1840,

BEING BISSEXTILE OR LEAP-YEAR, AND THE 64TH OF AMERICAN
INDEPENDENCE. CALCULATED FOR NEW YORK; ADAPTED
TO THE NORTHERN AND MIDDLE STATES.

Slave State *Free State*

NORTHERN HOSPITALITY—NEW YORK NINE MONTHS' LAW.
The slave steps out of the slave-state, and his chains fall. A free state, with another chain, stands ready to re-enslave him.

Thus saith the Lord, Deliver him that is spoiled out of the hands of the oppressor.

NEW YORK:
PUBLISHED BY THE AMERICAN ANTI-SLAVERY SOCIETY,
NO. 143 NASSAU STREET.

Clear the Track

In 1844, Jesse Hutchinson, a member of the Singing Hutchinson Family of New Hampshire - a staunchly militant Abolitionist group - wrote this song. The steam engine had just become a reality and the imagery of the railroad created tremendous excitement among listeners at their many concerts.

Music: Old Dan Tucker by Daniel D. Emmet

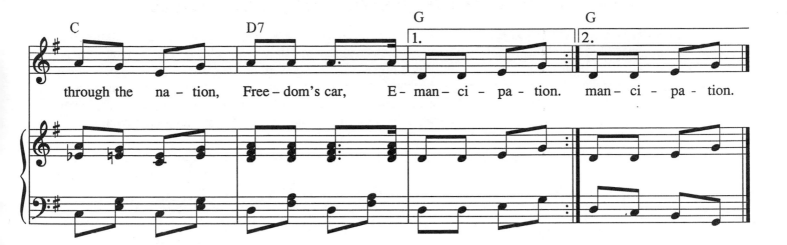

through the na – tion, Free – dom's car, E – man – ci – pa – tion. man – ci – pa – tion.

Men of various predilections,
Frightened, run in all directions;
Merchants, Editors, Physicians,
Lawyers, Priests and Politicians.
   Get out of the way! Every station, (3)
   Clear the track for 'mancipation.

All true friends of Emancipation,
Haste to Freedom's Railroad Station;
Quick into the cars get seated,
All is ready and completed.
   Put on the steam! All are crying, (3)
   And the Liberty Flags are flying.

Now again the Bell is tolling,
Soon you'll see the car wheels rolling;
Hinder not their destination,
Chartered for Emancipation.
   Wood up the fire! Keep it flashing, (3)
   While the train goes onward dashing.

Near the mighty car wheel's humming!
Now look out! *The Engine's coming!*
Church and Statesmen! Hear the thunder!
Clear the track! Or you'll fall under.
   Get off the track! All are singing, (3)
   While the Liberty Bell is ringing.

On triumphant, see them bearing,
Through sectarian rubbish tearing;
The Bell and Whistle and the Steaming
Startles thousands from their dreaming.
   Look out for the cars! While the Bell rings, (3)
   Ere the sound your funeral knell rings.

See the people run to meet us;
At the depots thousands greet us;
All take seats with exultation,
In the car Emancipation.
   Huzza! Huzza! Emancipation (3)
   Soon will bless our happy nation.

We Wait Beneath the Furnace Blast

In 1862, the Hutchinsons embarked on a singing trip to entertain the army of the Potomac. Their Abolitionist sentiments in general, and this song in particular, caused such an uproar that they were haled before General Kearny, who forbade them from performing before the army again. The controversy went up the chain of command, where it finally reached General McClellan, the commander of the army of the Potomac, who sustained the restrictive order. The offending song was finally brought before Lincoln, who said, "It is just the character of song that I desire the soldiers to hear." A compromise was worked out whereby the group could sing for troops upon the invitation of a specific commander.

Music: Ein Feste Burg (A Mighty Fortress Is Our God) by Martin Luther
Choral arrangement by J. S. Bach

The hand-breadth cloud the sages feared,
  Its bloody rain is dropping;
The poison plant the fathers spared,
  All else is overtopping.
    East, West, South, North,
    It curses the Earth;
    All justice dies,
    And fraud and lies
Live only in its shadow.

For who that leans on His right arm
  Was ever yet forsaken?
What righteous cause can suffer harm
  If He its part has taken?
    Though wild and loud,
    And dark the cloud,
    Behind its folds
    His hand upholds
The calm sky of tomorrow.

What gives the wheat fields blades of steel?
  What points the Rebel cannon?
What sets the roaring rabble's heel
  On the old star-spangled pennon?
    What breaks the oath
    Of the men of the South?
    What whets the knife
    For the Union's life?
Hark to the answer: SLAVERY!

Above the maddening cry for blood,
  Above the wild war-drumming,
Let Freedom's voice be heard, with good
  The evil overcoming.
    Give prayer and purse
    To stay The Curse,
    Whose wrong we share,
    Whose shame we bear,
Whose end shall gladden heaven!

Then waste no blows on lesser foes,
  In strife unworthy freemen;
God lifts today the veil, and shows
  The features of the demon!
    O North and South,
    Its victims both,
    Can ye not cry,
    "Let Slavery die!"
And Union find in freedom?

In vain the bells of war shall ring
  Of triumphs and revenges,
While still is spared the evil thing
  That severs and estranges.
    But blest the ear
    That yet shall hear
    The jubilant bell
    That rings the knell
Of Slavery forever!

What though the cast-out spirit tear
  The nation in his going?
We who have shared the guilt must share
  The pang of his o'erthrowing!
    Whate'er the loss,
    Whate'er the cross,
    Shall they complain
    Of present pain
Who trust in God's hereafter?

Then let the selfish lip be dumb,
  And hushed the breath of sighing;
Before the joy of peace must come
  The pains of purifying.
    God give us grace,
    Each in his place
    To bear his lot,
    And murmuring not,
Endure, and wait, and labor!

The Old Granite State

This was the "theme song" of the Hutchinsons. They opened every concert with it. In 1844, they were invited to sing for President John Tyler in the White House. They had intended to sing an anti-slavery verse as part of the song, but their congressman, John P. Hale, who had arranged their appearance, begged them not to include the offending verse. They complied, but as the Abolitionist struggle grew sharper, they added more and more anti-slavery songs to their concert programs. The reference to "Emancipation" and "Proclamation" in verse four was obviously added to the song much later.

We are all real Yankees,	Yes we're friends of Emancipation
We are all real Yankees,	And we'll sing the Proclamation
We are all real Yankees,	Till it echoes through our nation
From the Old Granite State.	From the Old Granite State.
And by prudent guessing,	That the tribe of Jesse,
And by prudent guessing,	That the tribe of Jesse,
And by prudent guessing,	That the tribe of Jesse,
We shall whittle through the world. *Chorus*	Are the friends of equal rights. *Chorus*
Liberty is our motto,	We are all Washingtonians,
Liberty is our motto,	Yes, we're all Washingtonians,
Equal liberty is our motto	Heav'n bless the Washingtonians,
In the Old Granite State.	Of the Old Granite State.
We despise oppression,	We are all teetotalers,
We despise oppression,	We are all teetotalers,
We despise oppression,	We are all teetotalers,
And we cannot be enslaved. *Chorus*	And have signed the Temp'rance Pledge. *Chorus*

Now three cheers altogether,
Shout Columbia's people ever,
Yankee hearts none can sever,
  In the Old Sister States.
Like our Sires before us,
We will swell the chorus,
Till the Heavens o'er us
  Shall resound the loud hussa.
    Hurrah! Hurrah! Hurrah! *Chorus*

Free Soil Chorus

The Free Soil Party emerged in 1848. They ran ex-President Martin Van Buren against Zachary Taylor. Their slogan was: Free Soil, Free Speech, Free Labor and Free Men.

Music: Old Lang Syne by Robert Burns

out   the shout to   all   a – bout, For___   free - dom and   free   soil.

We wage no bloody warfare here,
But gladly would we toil,
To show the South the matchless worth,
Of freedom and free soil.   *Chorus*

Nor care we aught for party names,
We ask not for the spoils.
But what we'll have is liberty,
For freemen and free soil. *Chorus*

Too long we've dwelt in party strife,
'Tis time to pour in oil,
So here's a dose for Uncle Sam,
Of freedom and free soil.   *Chorus*

The Civil War
1861-1865

Courtesy of New York Public Library Picture Collection

The Battle Cry of Freedom

This song was first introduced at a war rally in Chicago on July 24, 1862. It retained its popularity throughout the war, invariably being included in all wartime concerts and patriotic rallies. The Hutchinson family sang it at their concerts, and it was heard during the ceremonies at Fort Sumter on April 14, 1865, when the American flag was raised over the site of the first Union defeat.

Words and Music by George F. Root

Shout – ing the bat – tle cry of free – dom. The Un – ion for – ev – er, Hur –
rah, boys, hur-rah! Down with the trai – tor, Up with the star; While we
ral – ly 'round the flag, boys, ral – ly once a – gain,
Shout – ing the bat – tle cry of free – dom.

We are springing to the call of our brothers gone before,
   Shouting the battle cry of freedom,
And we'll fill the vacant ranks with a million freemen more,
   Shouting the battle cry of freedom. *Chorus*

We will welcome to our numbers the loyal, true, and brave,
   Shouting the battle cry of freedom,
And although they may be poor not a man shall be a slave,
   Shouting the battle cry of freedom. *Chorus*

So we're springing to the call from the East and from the West,
   Shouting the battle cry of freedom,
And we'll hurl the Rebel crew from the land we love the best,
   Shouting the battle cry of freedom. *Chorus*

The Battle Cry of Freedom, II (Battle Song)

We are marching to the field, boys,
We're going to the fight,
   Shouting the battle cry of freedom,
And we bear the glorious stars
For the Union and the right,
   Shouting the battle cry of freedom.

Chorus:
   The Union forever!
   Hurrah! Boys, hurrah!
   Down with the traitor,
   Up with the star.
   For we're marching to the field, boys,
   Going to the fight,
   Shouting the battle cry of freedom.

We will meet the Rebel host, boys,
With fearless heart and true,
   Shouting the battle cry of freedom,
And we'll show what Uncle Sam has
For loyal men to do,
   Shouting the battle cry of freedom. *Chorus*

If we fall amid the fray, boys,
We'll face them to the last,
   Shouting the battle cry of freedom,
And our comrades brave shall hear us
As they go rushing past,
   Shouting the battle cry of freedom. *Chorus*

Yes, for Liberty and Union
We're springing to the fight,
   Shouting the battle cry of freedom,
And the vict'ry shall be ours
For we're rising in our might,
   Shouting the battle cry of freedom. *Chorus*

The Battle Hymn of the Republic

Julia Ward Howe wrote the words to this most famous of all Civil War songs in November 1861, after hearing a group of soldiers singing "John Brown's Body." She and her husband, Dr. Samuel Howe of Boston, were active in the Abolitionist cause. It is believed that their Boston home was one of the "stations" of the Underground Railroad, which helped escaping Negro slaves get to Canada safely.

Mine eyes have seen the glo - ry of the

com - ing of the Lord; He is tram - pling out the vin - tage where the

grapes of wrath are stored; He hath loosed the fate - ful light - ning of His

ter - ri - ble swift sword, His truth is march - ing on.

I have seen Him in the watch fires of a hundred circling camps;
They have builded Him an altar in the evening dews and damps;
I can read His righteous sentence by the dim and flaring lamps,
His day is marching on. *Chorus*

I have read a fiery gospel writ in burnished rows of steel:
"As ye deal with My contemners, so with you My Grace shall deal;
Let the Hero, born of woman, crush the serpent with his heel,
Since God is marching on." *Chorus*

He has sounded forth the trumpet that shall never call retreat;
He is sifting out the hearts of men before His Judgment Seat;
Oh! be swift, my soul, to answer Him, be jubilant, my feet!
Our God is marching on. *Chorus*

In the beauty of the lilies Christ was born across the sea,
With a glory in his bosom that transfigures you and me;
As He died to make men holy, let us die to make men free,
While God is marching on. *Chorus*

John Brown's Body

On October 16, 1859, the fiery Abolitionist John Brown led a score of his followers on a suicidal attack upon the U.S. arsenal and armory at Harper's Ferry, Virginia. He had hoped that this raid would serve as a signal for a general slave uprising. That never happened, and less than 36 hours after it started, John Brown's impossible effort to free the slaves was over. He was captured by an attacking company of U.S. Marines under the command of Colonel Robert E. Lee.

Chorus

    Glory, glory, hallelujah,
    Glory, glory, hallelujah,
    Glory, glory, hallelujah,
    His soul goes marching on.

John Brown's body lies a-mouldering in the grave,
John Brown's body lies a-mouldering in the grave,
John Brown's body lies a-mouldering in the grave,
But his soul goes marching on.

He's gone to be a soldier in the Army of the Lord...
His soul goes marching on. *Chorus*

John Brown's knapsack is strapped upon his back...
His soul goes marching on. *Chorus*

John Brown died that the slaves might be free...
But his soul goes marching on. *Chorus*

The stars above in Heaven now are looking
  kindly down...
On the grave of old John Brown. *Chorus*

Courtesy of New York Public Library Picture Collection

Tenting on the Old Camp Ground

Walter Kittredge wrote this song in 1863, while preparing to answer the draft call he had received. He was exempted from military service, however, due to reasons of health. Kittredge was a member of one of the many Hutchinson Family singing groups. When the Hutchinsons heard the song they immediately added it to their repertoire. It was an instantaneous success.

We're tent – ing to- night on the old camp ground, Give us a song to

cheer Our wea – ry hearts, a song of home And friends we love so

dear. *Chorus* Man-y are the hearts that are wea-ry to – night,

We've been tenting tonight on the old camp ground,
Thinking of days gone by,
Of the loved ones at home that gave us the hand,
And the tear that said, "Goodbye!" *Chorus*

We are tired of war on the old camp ground,
Many are dead and gone,
Of the brave and true who've left their homes,
Others been wounded long. *Chorus*

We've been fighting today on the old camp ground,
Many are lying near;
Some are dead and some are dying,
Many are in tears.

Final Chorus:
Many are the hearts that are weary tonight,
Wishing for the war to cease;
Many are the hearts that are looking for the right
To see the dawn of peace.
   Dying tonight, dying tonight,
   Dying on the old camp ground.

101

Roll, Alabama, Roll

The Confederate gunboat *Alabama* was built in Birkenhead, England, in 1862. It was intended to counter the Union blockade of Confederate ports. For some two years it preyed upon Northern shipping, sinking and capturing some 56 merchant vessels. On June 19, 1865, the *U.S.S. Kearsarge* finally caught up with and sank the *Alabama* outside the French port of Cherbourg.

When the Al — a — bam — a's keel was laid,

Roll, Al — a–bam — a, roll, 'Twas __ laid in the yard of

Jon–a–than Laird, Oh, roll, Al — a–bam — a, roll.

'Twas laid in the yard of Jonathan Laird,
  Roll, *Alabama*, roll.
'Twas laid in the town of Birkenhead,
  Oh, roll, *Alabama*, roll.

Down the Mersey ways she rolled then,
  Roll, *Alabama*, roll.
Liverpool fitted her with guns and men,
  Oh, roll, *Alabama*, roll.

From the Western Isles she sailed forth,
    Roll, *Alabama,* roll,
To destroy the commerce of the North,
    Oh, roll, *Alabama,* roll.

To Cherbourg port she sailed one day,
    Roll, *Alabama,* roll,
To take her count of prize money,
    Oh, roll, *Alabama,* roll.

Many a sailor lad he saw his doom,
    Roll, *Alabama,* roll,
When the *Ke-arsarge* it hove in view,
    Oh, roll, *Alabama,* roll.

'Til a ball from the forward pivot that day,
    Roll, *Alabama,* roll,
Shot the *Alabama's* stern away,
    Oh, roll, *Alabama,* roll.

Off the three-mile limit in sixty-five,
    Roll, *Alabama,* roll,
The *Alabama* went to her grave,
    Oh, roll, *Alabama,* roll.

Alabama going down, June 19, 1864

Officers of the *Kearsarge* assembled on her deck, 1864

When Johnny Comes Marching Home

Patrick S. Gilmore was bandmaster of the Union Army in New Orleans. The unmistakable Irish quality of this song is no doubt due to Gilmore's Irish birth. However, no evidence has ever been produced that would conclusively show a specific Irish antecedent to "Johnny." What we know for certain is that soldiers in both armies sang and identified with "Johnny."

By Patrick S. Gilmore

John – ny comes march – ing home a – gain, Hur – rah,_____ hur –

rah!_____ We'll give him a heart – y wel – come then, Hur – rah,_____ hur–

The old church bell will peal with joy,
  Hurrah, hurrah!
To welcome home our darling boy,
  Hurrah, hurrah!
The village lads and lassies say,
With roses they will strew the way,
And we'll all feel gay when Johnny comes
    marching home.

Get ready for the Jubilee,
  Hurrah, hurrah!
We'll give the hero three times three,
  Hurrah, hurrah!
The laurel wreath is ready now
To place upon his loyal brow,
And we'll all feel gay when Johnny comes
    marching home.

Let love and friendship on that day,
  Hurrah, hurrah!
Their choicest treasures then display,
  Hurrah, hurrah!
And let each one perform some part,
To fill with joy the warrior's heart,
And we'll all feel gay when Johnny comes marching home.

Transportation

The E-Ri-E Canal

Twenty years after New York Governor De Witt Clinton floated down the newly opened Erie Canal on the *Sequoia Chief* from Buffalo to Albany, and down the Hudson River to New York harbor in 1825, Michigan had increased its population by sixty times and Ohio had climbed from thirteenth to the third most heavily populated state in the Union. The Erie Canal was the highway for most of these settlers and their goods. Clinton's 425-mile ditch had proved itself. New York was, indeed, the Empire State.

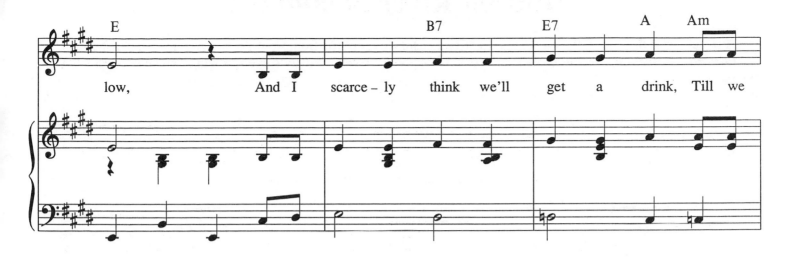

low,　　　And I　scarce – ly　think　we'll　get　a　drink,　Till we

get　to　Buf – fa　—　lo – o　—　o,　till　we　get　to　Buf – fa – lo.

We were loaded down with barley,
We were chock full up on rye,
And the captain he looked down at me
With his gol-durn wicked eye. *Chorus*

The captain he came up on deck
With a spyglass in his hand.
And the fog it was so gosh-darn thick,
That he could not spy the land. *Chorus*

Two days out of Syracuse
Our vessel struck a shoal,
And we like to all been drownded
On a chunk o' Lackawanna coal. *Chorus*

Our cook she was a grand old gal,
She wore a ragged dress.
We hoisted her upon a pole
As a signal of distress. *Chorus*

The captain, he got married
And the cook, she went to jail.
And I'm the only son of a gun
That's left to tell the tale. *Chorus*

Hudson River Steamboat

A picture of 19th-century life on the Hudson River: Busy river traffic from New York to Albany...shad fishermen (a major occupation)...pickle boats from Yonkers supplying New York City's ever-growing demand... steamboat races...

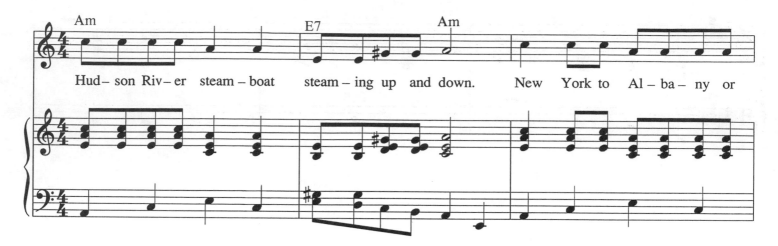

Hud– son Riv–er steam–boat steam–ing up and down. New York to Al–ba–ny or

an – y ri – ver town. Choo – choo to go a – head, choo – choo to back 'er, The

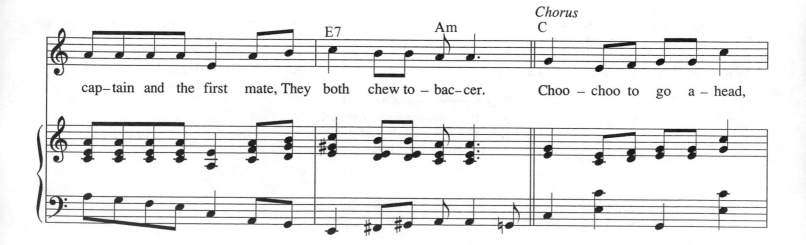

cap–tain and the first mate, They both chew to – bac–cer. Choo – choo to go a – head,

choo – choo to slack 'er, Pack –et boat, tow boat and a doub –le stack– er.

Choo-choo to Tar-ry-town, Spuy –ten Duy-vil all a– round. Choo-choo to go a– head, choo– choo to back er.

Shad boat, pickle boat, lying side by side,
Fisherfolk and sailormen, waiting for the tide,
Rain cloud, storm cloud over yonder hill,
Thunder on the Dunderberg, rumbles in the kill. *Chorus*

The *Sedgewick* was racing and she lost all hope,
Used up her steam on the big calliope,
But she hopped right along, she was hopping quick,
All the way from Stony Point up to Pappaloppen Crick.

Final Chorus
Choo, choo to go ahead,
Choo, choo, to slack 'er.
Packet boat, tow boat and a double stacker.
New York to Albany, Rondout and Tivoli,
Choo, choo, to go ahead,
And choo, choo to back 'er.

The Titanic

On the night of April 14–15, 1912, the "unsinkable" ocean liner *Titanic* struck an iceberg off the Grand Banks of Newfoundland on her maiden voyage and sank with a loss of 1,513 lives. The disaster shocked and astounded the world. This song, however, is generally sung in a rousing, almost good-natured manner.

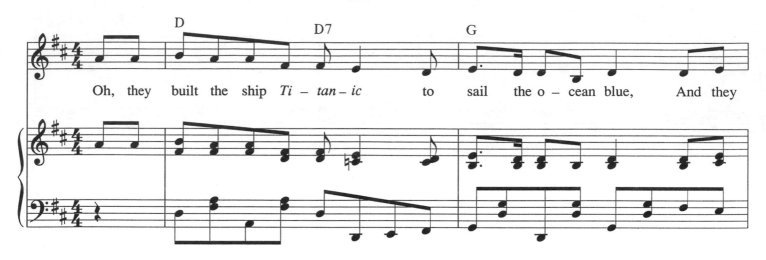

Oh, they built the ship Ti – tan – ic to sail the o – cean blue, And they

thought they had a ship that the wa–ter would nev – er go through; But the

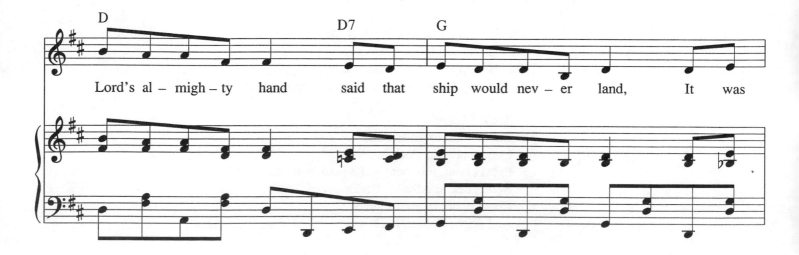

Lord's al – migh – ty hand said that ship would nev – er land, It was

Oh, they sailed from England's shore
'Bout a thousand miles or more,
When the rich refused to associate with the poor
So, they put them down below,
Where they'd be the first to go,
It was sad when that great ship went down. *Chorus*

Oh, the boat was full of sin,
And the sides about to burst,
When the captain shouted, "Women and children first!"
Oh, the captain tried to wire,
But the lines were all on fire,
It was sad when that great ship went down. *Chorus*

Oh, they swung the lifeboats out
O'er the deep and raging sea,
And the band struck up with "A-nearer, My God, to Thee."
Little children wept and cried,
As the waves swept o'er the side,
It was sad when that great ship went down. *Chorus*

The Ox-Driving Song

Sometimes it is hard to pinpoint the exact locale of a song, even if a place name is mentioned. There is a Saluda in southwestern North Carolina in the Blue Ridge range of the Appalachians. It is not too hard to imagine a tough old ox-driver whipping his team into "Saluda-o"; but, when you sing it, it comes out "Saludio."

I pop my whip and I bring the blood, I make my lead – ers

take the mud. _____ I grab the wheel _____ and I turn them a –

round; _____ One long, long pull and we're on high ground. To my

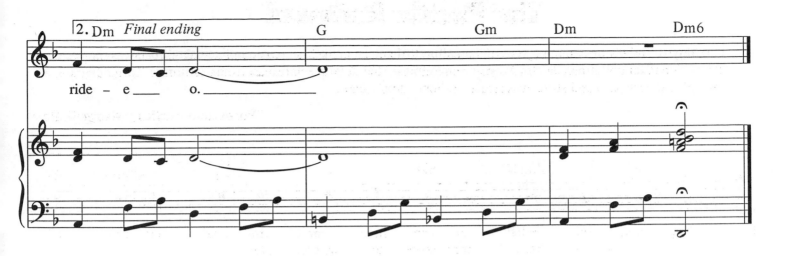

Chorus
To my roll, to my roll to my ride-e-o,
To my roll, to my roll to my ride-e-o,
To my ride-e-o, to my ru-de-o,
To my roll, to my roll, to my ride-e-o.

On the fourteenth day of October-o,
I hitched my team in order-o,
To drive the hills of Saludio -
To me roll, to me roll, to me ri-de-o.   *Chorus*

When I got there the hills were steep,
'Twould make tenderhearted people weep
To hear me cuss and pop my whip,
To see my oxen pull and slip.   *Chorus*

When I get home I'll have revenge,
I'll land my family among my friends.
I'll bid adieu to the whip and line,
And drive no more in the wintertime.   *Chorus*

The Pacific Railroad

On May 10, 1869, after some six years of incredibly difficult labor, the first trans-continental railroad was completed. The Union Pacific Railroad laid track west from Nebraska; the Central Pacific east from California. The golden spike that joined these two steel strips was struck at Promontory, Utah.

Words and Music by George F. Root

We who but yesterday appeared
As settlers of the border,
Where only savages were reared
'Mid chaos and disorder;
We wake to find ourselves midway
In continental station,
And send our greetings either way
Across the mighty nation. *Chorus*

We reach out towards the Golden Gate,
And eastward to the oceans;
The tea will come at lightning rate,
And likewise Yankee notions.
From spicy islands of the West,
The breezes now are blowing,
And all the world will do its best
To keep the cars a-going. *Chorus*

Bill McCandless' Ride

"A loaded furniture van roared out of control down the steepest part of Nob Hill today, killing seven persons. The big truck gained a speed estimated at 100 miles an hour as it crossed the main street of Chinatown. . . . William R. McCandless . . . of Davenport, Iowa, driver of the van stayed with the vehicle all the way. . . . He swerved to avoid other cars as he pounded on a mute horn. . . . His helper, Wayne de Wolf . . . unfamiliar with the rig . . . looked vainly for the emergency brakes and then leaped at the instruction of his companion. . . ." (*The New York Times, May 27, 1955; Dateline: San Francisco*)

By Jerry Silverman (1955)

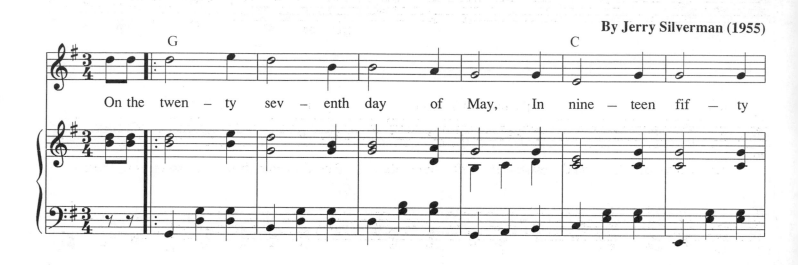

On the twen — ty sev — enth day of May, In nine — teen fif — ty

five,_____ A truck ran wild in Fris — co town, and snuffed out

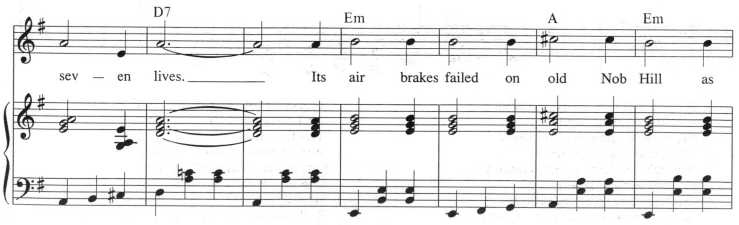

sev — en lives._____ Its air brakes failed on old Nob Hill as

it was start—ing down,_____ And at one hun—dred miles an

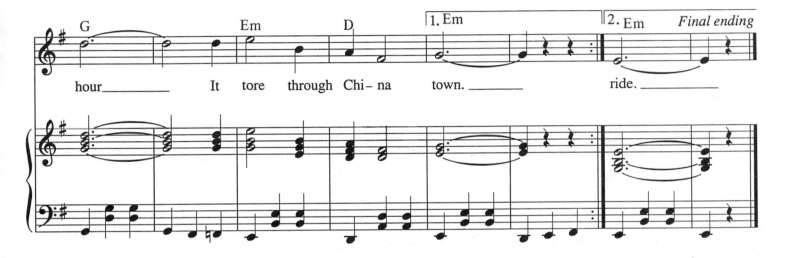

hour_____ It tore through Chi—na town._____ ride._____

William R. McCandless,
The driver of the van,
Stayed with it all down the hill,
And there died like a man.
He called out to his helper then,
Said, "Wayne, my brakes are gone.
You'd better jump and save yourself,
For I can't hold on long."

The truck picked up speed and then began
McCandless' terrible ride.
He know he was doomed, but to save other lives
He swerved from side to side.
Pounding on a horn that was mute,
He tried to stop the truck.
But he must have known as down he roared,
That he would have no luck.

Clay Street was crowded with people that day,
As the ten-ton truck sped down.
And when its awful course was run,
Six bodies lay on the ground.
Then there came a terrible crash,
As the van hit the front of a store.
When the police and firemen came they saw
McCandless would drive no more.

Take warning, all you drivers,
Take warning in good time ——
Remember Bill McCandless,
Who drove the Mayflower line.
Like Casey Jones he stuck to his post,
And at his wheel he died,
And when songs of working heroes are sung,
We'll sing of McCandless' ride.

The Bigler

According to the story, the *Bigler* was the slowest vessel on the Great Lakes. You can plot its course from Milwaukee to Detroit from verse to verse. "Wabbleshanks," in the fourth verse, is sailorese for Waugoshance Point, at the entrance to the Straits of Makinac ("Makinaw") — heading east from Lake Michigan into Lake Huron.

Come all my boys and lis–ten, _____ a song I'll sing to you. _____ It's

all a–bout the Big–ler — and of her jol–ly crew. In Mil–wau–kee last Oc–

to – ber we chanced to get a sight In the schoon–er called the

It was on one Sunday morning, just at the hour of ten,
When the *Nickle Roberts* towed the *Bigler* into Lake Michigan,
O there we made our canvas in the middle of the fleet,
O the wind hauled to the south'ard, boys, and we had to give her sheet. *Chorus*

The wind come down from the sou' sou'-west, it blowed both stiff and strong,
You had orter seen the *Bigler* as she plowed Lake Michigan,
O far beyant her foaming bows the fiery waves to fling,
With every stitch of canvas and her course was wing and wing. *Chorus*

We made Beaver Head Light and Wabbleshanks, the entrance to the straits,
And might have passed the whole fleet there, if they'd hove to and wait,
But we drove them all before us the nicest you ever saw,
Clear out into Lake Huron through the Straits of Mackinaw! *Chorus*

First, Forty Mile Point and Presque Isle Light, and then we boomed away,
The wind being fresh and fair, for the Isle of Thunder Bay;
The wind it shifted to a close haul, all on the starboard tack,
With a good lookout ahead we made for Point Aubarques. *Chorus*

We made the light and kept in sight of Michigan's east shore
A-booming for the river as we'd often done before,
And when abreast Port Huron Light, our small anchor we let go,
The tug *Kate Moffet* came along and took the *Bigler* in tow. *Chorus*

The *Moffet* took six schooners in tow, and all of us fore and aft,
She took us down to Lake Saint Claire and stuck us on the flat,
She parted the *Hunter's* towline in trying to give relief,
And stem to stern went the *Bigler,* smash into the *Mapleleaf. Chorus*

Then she towed us through and left us outside the river light,
Lake Erie for to wander and the blustering winds to fight.
The wind was from the sou'west, and we paddled our own canoe,
Her jib boom pointed the dummy, she's hellbent for Buffalo. *Chorus*

Women's Rights

Winning The Vote

(A Musical Colloquy)

The struggle for woman suffrage in America is actually older than our country. The first recorded demand for votes for women was made by Margaret Brent in Maryland in 1647. For the next two hundred years, however, woman suffrage remained a minor issue as America fought the battle for national independence. The next important step forward in the woman suffrage movement came with the emergence of the great anti-slavery agitation of the 1830s and 1840s. The natural ideological affinity of the two causes was heightened by the active and leading role played by many women in the Abolitionist movement....With the end of the Civil War...the suffrage movement took a gigantic leap ahead. It became apparent to the leading women's rights advocates that the key issue was suffrage. Accordingly, in 1869, Elizabeth Stanton and Susan B. Anthony helped to found the National Woman Suffrage Association under the inspiration of Lucy Stone and Julia Ward Howe....At the great national suffrage conventions, at the historic parades and public demonstrations...the singing suffragettes chanted a melody of equal rights which unmistakably caught the ear of the nation... *(Sing Out,* Vol. 6, No. 4, 1957)

Words by Mrs. A. B. Smith (1912)

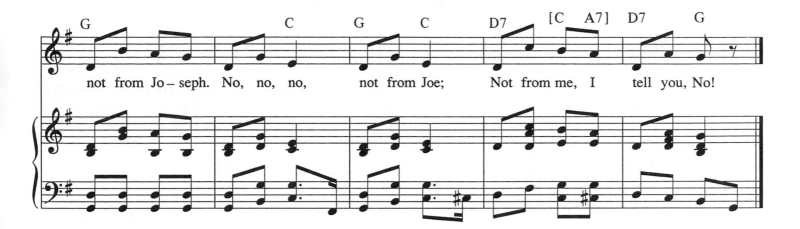

not from Jo—seph. No, no, no, not from Joe; Not from me, I tell you, No!

Girls: Say, friend Joseph, why not we should vote as well as you?
  Are there no problems in the State that need our wisdom, too?
  We must pay our taxes same as you; as citizens be true,
  And if some wicked thing we do, to jail we're sent by you.
  Yes we are, same as you;
  And you know it, don't you, Joseph?
  Yes, you do, yet you boast:
  You'll not help us win the vote.

Boys: But dear women, can't you see, the home is your true sphere?
  Just think of going to the polls perhaps two times a year.
  You are wasting time you ought to use in sewing and at work,
  Your home neglected all those hours; would you such duties shirk?
  Help from Joe? Help from Joe:
  If he knows it, not from Joseph;
  No, no, no, not from Joe!
  Not from me, I tell you no!

Girls: Joseph, tell us something new — we're tired of that old song.
  We'll sew the seams and cook the meals, to vote won't take us long.
  We will help to clean house — the one too large for man to clean alone,
  The State and Nation, don't you see, when we the vote have won.
  Yes we will, and you'll help,
  For you'll need our help, friend Joseph.
  Yes you will, when we're in,
  So you'd better help us win.

Boys: You're just right — how blind I've been, I ne'er had seen it thus;
  'Tis true that taxes you must pay without a word of fuss.
  You are subject to the laws men made, and yet no word or note,
  Can you sing out where it will count. I'll help you win the vote!
  Yes, I will.

Girls: Thank you, Joe.

All: We'll together soon be voters.
  Yes we will, if you'll all
  Vote "Yes" at the polls next fall.

Keep Woman In Her Sphere

"Keeping woman in her sphere" was a favorite know- nothing 19th-century expression which literally meant the imprisonment of women in the home.

Music: Old Lang Syne by Robert Burns

I have a neigh – bor, one of those not___ ver – y hard to find, Who know it all with out de – bate, And___ nev – er change their mind. I asked him, "What of wo – men's rights?" He said in tones se – vere: "My

mind on that is all made up, Keep___ wo — man in her sphere.

I saw a man in tattered garb
Forth from the grog-shop come.
He squandered all his cash for drink,
And starved his wife at home,
I asked him, "Should not women vote?"
He answered with a sneer,
"I've taught my wife to know her place,
 Keep woman in her sphere."

I met an earnest, thoughtful man,
Not many days ago,
Who pondered deep all human law,
The honest truth to know.
I asked him, "What of woman's cause?"
The answer came sincere,
"Her rights are just the same as mine,
 Let woman choose her sphere."

Courtesy of New York Public Library Picture Collection

Let Us All Speak Our Minds

It took 71 years, from the national woman's suffrage convention in 1848 to the final enactment of the 19th Amendment to the Constitution, for American women to win the right to vote. The struggle was a long, slow and often bitter one, marked by ever-growing support for women's rights and vitriolic opposition. And uniting the embattled suffragists in dramatic demonstrations and buoying up dashed hopes in the midst of setbacks and despair was one of the traditional weapons of every American movement for social progress — song!

Music by William Brough
Words by J. G. Maeder

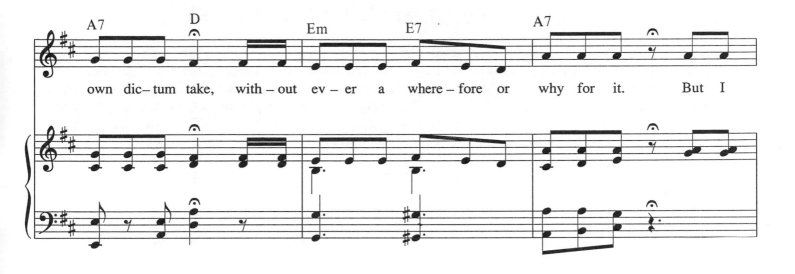

own dic–tum take, with – out ev – er a where–fore or why for it. But I

don't and I can't, and I won't and I shan't; No I will speak my mind if I die for it.

For we know it's all fudge to say man's the best judge
Of what should be and shouldn't, and so on.
That woman should bow, nor attempt to say how
She considers that matters should go on.
I never yet gave up myself thus a slave,
However my husband might try for it;
For I can't and I won't and I sha'n't and I don't,
But I will speak my mind if I die for it.

Bread and Roses

"New Year's Day, 1912, ushered in one of the most historic struggles in the history of the American working class. On that cold January first, the textile workers of Lawrence, Massachusetts, began a nine-week strike which shook the very foundations of the Bay State and had national repercussions. In its last session, the Massachusetts State Legislature, after tremendous pressure from the workers, had finally passed a law limiting the working hours of children under the age of 18 to 54 hours a week. Needless to say, the huge textile corporations had viciously opposed the law. As an act of retaliation, the employers cut the working hours of all employees to 54 hours a week, with a commensurate cut in wages, of course. The workers in the Lawrence factories, some 35,000 of them, answered this with a complete walk-out. . . . During a parade through Lawrence, a group of women workers carried banners proclaiming 'Bread and Roses!' This poetic presentation of the demands of women workers for equal pay for equal work, together with special consideration as women, echoed throughout the country." (*Sing Out,* Vol. 2, No. 7, 1957)

Music by Martha Coleman
Words by James Oppenhein

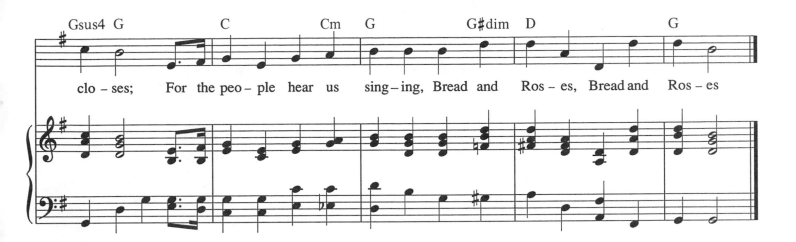

clo – ses; For the peo – ple hear us sing – ing, Bread and Ros – es, Bread and Ros – es

As we come marching, marching, we battle too, for men,
For they are women's children and we mother them again.
Our lives shall not be sweated from birth until life closes.
Hearts starve as well as bodies:
Give us bread, but give us roses.

As we come marching, marching, unnumbered women dead
Go crying through our singing their ancient song of bread.
Small art and love and beauty their drudging spirits knew.
Yes, it is bread that we fight for,
But we fight for roses, too.

As we come marching, marching, we bring the Greater Days,
The rising of the women means the rising of the race.
No more the drudge and idler, ten that toil where one reposes,
But a sharing of life's glories,
Bread and Roses, Bread and Roses.

Courtesy of New York Public Library Picture Collection

Courtesy of New York Public Library Picture Collection

The Spanish-American War and the Philippine Insurrection 1898-1901

Courtesy of New York Public Library Picture Collection

The Battleship of Maine

On the 15th of February, 1898, the U.S. battleship *Maine* was destroyed in Havana harbor by an explosion, with a loss of 260 lives. The cry of "Remember the *Maine!*" was taken up all across the United States. On the 20th of April, President McKinley approved a resolution demanding the withdrawal of Spain from its Cuban colony. On the 22nd the President declared a blockade of Cuban ports. On the 24th the Spanish government declared war—a war that would stretch from Cuba all the way to the Philippines.

Mc—Kin—ley called for vol—un—teers, Then I got my gun. First
Span—iard I saw com—ing, I dropped my gun and run; It was
all a—bout__ that Bat—tle—ship of Maine. At war with that great na—tion
Spain. When I get back from Spain I want to

hon – or my name. It was all a – bout__ that Bat – tle – ship of Maine.

Why are you running,
Are you afraid to die?
The reason that I'm running
Is because I cannot fly.
It was all about that Battleship of Maine. *Chorus*

The blood was a-running
And I was running, too.
I give me feet good exercise,
I had nothing else to do.
It was all about that Battleship of Maine. *Chorus*

When they were a-chasing me,
I fell down on my knees.
First thing I cast my eyes upon
Was a great big pot of peas.
It was all about that Battleship of Maine. *Chorus*

The peas they was greasy,
The meat it was fat,
The boys was fighting Spaniards,
While I was fighting that.
It was all about that Battleship of Maine. *Chorus*

What kind of shoes
Do the rough riders wear?
Buttons on the side,
Cost five and a half a pair.
It was all about that Battleship of Maine. *Chorus*

What kind of shoes
Do the poor farmers wear?
Worn-out old brogans,
Cost a dollar a pair.
It was all about that Battleship of Maine. *Chorus*

Courtesy of New York Public Library Picture Collection

In Mindanao

Admiral Dewey sailed his fleet into Manila harbor in May 1898. By August the "liberation" of the Philippines was complete. Almost immediately friction, and then hostilities, broke out between the American forces and Philippine rebel leader Emilio Aguinaldo. For the next three years there was fighting between the U.S. Army and Aguinaldo's troops. With the capture of Aguinaldo on March 23, 1901, the "Philippine Insurrection" was effectively terminated. This song describes the difficulties the U.S. Army encountered in building a strategic road on the island of Mindanao.

We – said good—bye to the brown ba—baye in Na – ic and – San—ta Cruz, _____ And for Min – da – nao we took our vow in a glass of foam – ing___ booze. We're— camped in the sand of a

for – eign land, By the migh – ty A – gus Riv – er; With the

brush at your toes and the "skee–ters"at your nose, And a kris, per – haps, in your liv – er.

We've the dhobee-itch and the hamstring hitch,
 The jimjams and the fever;
The ping-pong wrist and the bolo fist,
 And a bumpus on the liver.
We're going up to Lake Lanao,
 To the town they call Marahui;
When the road is built and the Moros "kilt,"
 There'll none of us be sorry.

We're blasting stumps and grading bumps;
 Our hands and backs are sore, oh!
We work all day just dreaming of our pay,
 And damn the husky Moros!
When you're pulled from bed with a great big head,
 And a weakness o'er you stealing;
The sick report is a fine resort
 To cure that tired feeling.

The Carabao

The carabao, or water buffalo, was the "patron saint" of the Military Order of the Carabao, an organization of officers of the army and navy who served in the Philippines during the insurrection. It is the principal beast of burden in the Islands. It is not known for its speed.

Music: Oh Tannenbaum

Oh! Ca – ra – bao, old Ca – ra – bao,_____ Be – fore they e'er could strike a blow, In – vad – ing ar – mies must a – wait _____ up-on thy slow and meas – ured gait. For who can say that in his hand A – bides the pow'r at thy com – mand? 'Tis

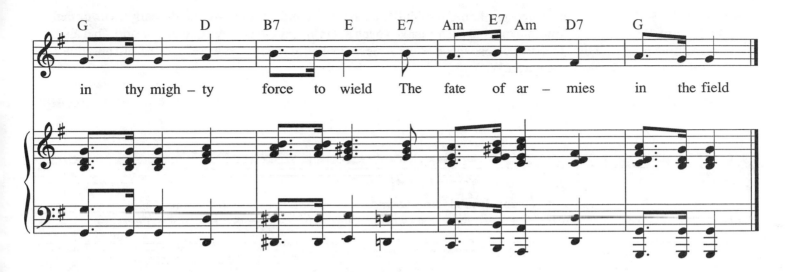

in thy migh – ty force to wield The fate of ar – mies in the field

Oh! Carabao, Old Carabao,
Great monarch of the road art thou!
Thy value rests in merit plain,
Old toiler through the mud and rain.

Well bearest thou thy lowly part,
No weakness knows thy giant heart;
With thy broad horn a single blow,
Well could'st thou lay thy master low.

Yet all thy strength thou bindest still
To slave and suffer at his will;
And steady, draw the weary load,
Till death o'ertakes thee on the road.

Oh! Carabao, Old Carabao,
Well could we place upon thy brow
A laurel wreath for work well done
In driving storm and scorching sun.

Stung Right

Joe Hill (1879–1915) was the composer of dozens of militant labor and political songs during the early years of the 20th century. Here he takes ironic aim not only at the naive young man who joins the navy "to see the world," but also at the Armour meat packing company, whose spoiled cans of meat supplied to U.S. forces were the cause of a notorious scandal during the Spanish–American War.

By Joe Hill

The man, he said, "The U. S. Fleet, it is no place for slaves,
"For everything you have to do is stand and watch the waves!"
But in the morn, at five o'clock, they woke me from my snooze,
To scrub the deck and polish brass, and shine the captain's shoes! *Chorus*

One day a dude in uniform to me began to shout;
I simply plugged him in the jaw, and knocked him down and out;
They slammed me right in irons then and said, "You are a case."
On bread and water then I lived for twenty-seven days. *Chorus*

One day the captain said, "Today I'll show you something nice,
"All hands line up, we'll go ashore and do some exercise."
He made us run for seven miles as fast as we could run,
And with a packing on our back that weighed a half a ton. *Chorus*

Some time ago when Uncle Sam he had a war with Spain,
And many of the boys in blue were in the battle slain,
Not all were killed by bullets, though; no, not by any means,
The biggest part that were killed by Armour's pork and beans. *Chorus*

Courtesy of New York Public Library Picture Collection

World War I
1914-1918

When I Lay Down

There was a $10,000 life insurance policy issued to each American soldier fighting in France during World War I from 1916 to 1918.

I only want to live but I know I've got to die,
The fun I'll have be in the sweet by and by;
Oh, this man's war is a mean man's war for sure.

All of those mamas back home are a-pinin'
For a papa like me when the moon is a-shinin';
Oh, this man's war is mean man's war for sure.

Can't think about livin' when you know you got to die,
Can't think about lovin' when the Heinie's nearby;
Oh, this man's war is a mean man's war for sure.

Findin' out every day how to be a fighter,
I'm a-totin' my gun but my pack's gettin' lighter;
Oh, this man's dwar is mean man's war for sure.

There's a sniper over yonder in what's left of a tree,
But he'll be a snipin' son of a gun before he ever snipes me;
Oh, this man's war is a mean man's war for sure.

New York 1919   Courtesy of New York Public Library Picture Collection

Deep Sea Blues

For many American soldiers, the trip over to France by troop ship afforded them their first glimpse of the Atlantic Ocean.

Words traditional
Music by Jerry Silverman

aw – ful sail – in', wail – in', Got those aw – ful deep – sea blues.____

Sol – diers down be – low lay – in' cold and dead,____
All these col – ored sol – diers go – in' out to France,____

Ev – 'ry bo – dy 'cept me.____
All these sol – diers and me.____

Drop 'em ov – er – board
Gon – na help the whites

load – ed down with lead.____ while we're at sea.____ Oh,
make the Kai – ser dance.____ Just wait an' see.____ Oh,

Coast Artillery Song

For an "official" look at the war, comes the "Coast Artillery Song," published in *The Army Song Book,* which was compiled by the Commission on Training Camp Activities.

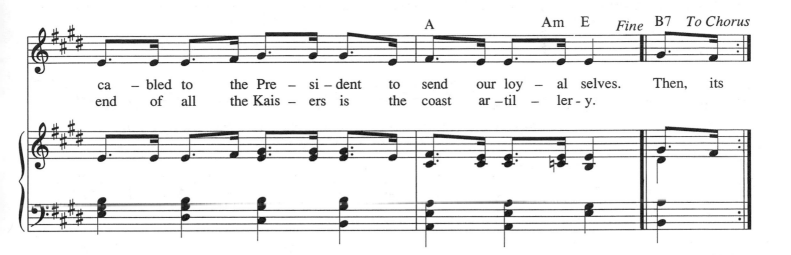

ca – bled to the Pre – si – dent to send our loy – al selves. Then, its
end of all the Kais – ers is the coast ar –til – ler - y.

When British Tommies took the field to stop the barb' rous Hun,
They found their light artillery was beaten, gun for gun,
So Marshal French got on the wire and quickly told the king
That the garrison artillery would be the only thing. *Chorus*

So limber up the sixes and tens and other ones,
And bracket on the O. T. line until you get the Huns
There may be many plans and schemes to set this old world free,
But you'll find in every one a part for coast artillery. *Chorus*

149

That Crazy War

A veteran of the American Army in France in 1917 looks back and wonders about the coming of World War II in the unsettling period of the 1930s.

Now, o – ver there a — cross the sea they're got an – oth – er

war. But oh, I won – der if they know just what they're fight – ing

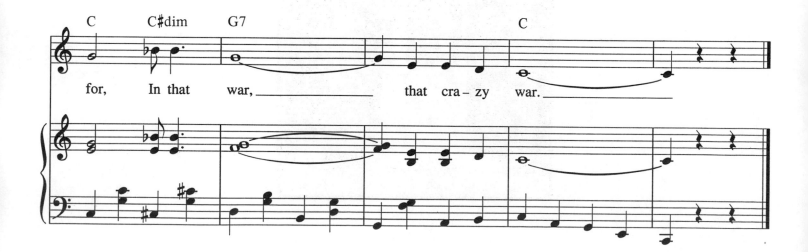

for, In that war,_____ that cra – zy war._____

In nineteen-seventeen, you know,
We helped them win their fight,
But all we got what a lesson
In what Sherman said was right,
　In that war, that crazy war.

I was a simple country lad,
I lived down on the farm.
I'd never even killed a gnat,
Nor done a body harm,
　Until that war, that crazy war.

One day the sheriff caught me,
Said, "Come along, my son,
Your Uncle Sam is needing you
To help him tote a gun,
　In that war, that crazy war."

They took me to the courthouse,
My head was in a whirl,
And when the doctors passed on me,
I wished I'd been a girl,
　In that war, that crazy war.

They took me to the rifle range
To hear the bullets sing.
I shot and shot that whole day long
And never hit a thing,
　In that war, that crazy war.

The captain said to fire at will,
And I said, "Who is he?"
The old fool got so raving mad,
He fired his gun at me,
　In that war, that crazy war.

When first we got to sunny France,
I looked around with glee,
But rain and kil-o-meters
Was all that I could see,
　In that war, that crazy war.

A cannonball flew overhead,
I started home right then.
The corporal was after me,
But the general beat us in,
　In that war, that crazy war.

And now we're back at home again
From over there in France,
The enemy lost the battle
And we lost all our pants,
　In that war, that crazy war.

I run all over Europe,
A-trying to save my life.
There'll come another war,
I'll send my darling wife,
　To that war, that crazy war.

Well, wars may come and wars may go,
But get this on your mind,
There will come another war,
And I'll be hard to find,
　In that war, that crazy war.

Courtesy of New York Public Library Picture Collection

Courtesy of New York Public Library Picture Collection

The Labor Movement
1900–1935

Courtesy of New York Public Library Picture Collection

Casey Jones-The Union Scab

Joe Hill wrote "Casey Jones" in 1911 as a topical comment on a strike of Southern Pacific railroad workers in California.

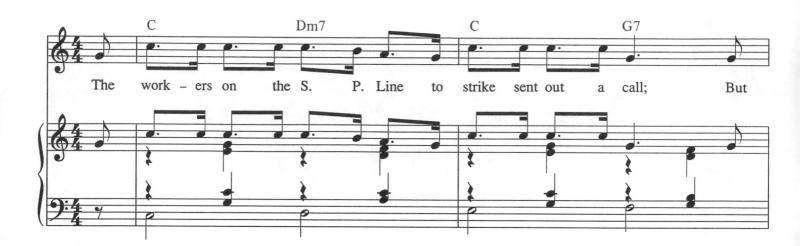

The work – ers on the S. P. Line to strike sent out a call; But

Ca – sey Jones, the en – gi – neer, he would – n't strike at all. His

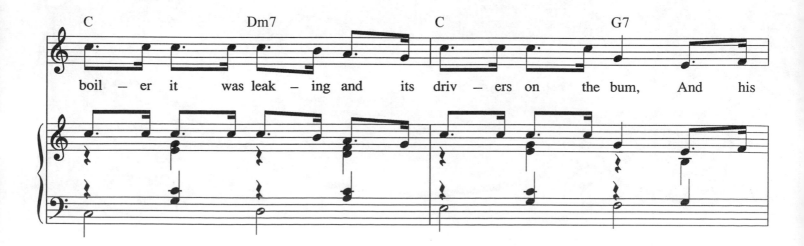

boil — er it was leak – ing and its driv – ers on the bum, And his

The workers said to Casey, "Won't you help us win this strike?"
But Casey said, "Let me alone. You'd better take a hike!"
Then Casey's wheezy engine ran right off the worn-out track,
And Casey hit the river with an awful crack.
    Casey Jones hit the river bottom,
    Casey Jones broke his blooming spine.
    Casey Jones became an angeleno,
    And took a trip to heaven on the S. P. Line.

When Casey Jones got up to heaven— to the Pearly Gate,
He said, "I'm Casey Jones, the guy that pulled the S. P. freight."
"You're just the man," said Peter. "Our musicians are on strike;
You can get a job a-scabbing anytime you like."
    Casey Jones got a job in heaven,
    Casey Jones was doing mighty fine.
    Casey Jones went a-scabbing on the angels,
    Just like he did to workers on the S. P. Line.

The angels got together and they said it wasn't fair
For Casey Jones to go around a-scabbing everywhere.
The angels union Local Twenty-Three it sure was there,
And they promptly fired Casey down the Golden Stair.
    Casey Jones went to hell a-flying,
    "Casey Jones," the devil said, "oh fine.
    Casey Jones, get busy shoveling sulphur;
    That's what you get for scabbing on the S. P. Line."

The Death of Harry Simms

The coal-mining counties of Kentucky were scenes of extreme violence directed against striking miners in the early 1930s. Harry Simms was a young organizer for the National Miners Union who was gunned down near Pineville, Kentucky. He was on his way to collect truckloads of food and clothing which had been donated from out of state to aid the Brush Creek miners who were on strike. "Aunt" Molly Jackson, who wrote this with her brother, Jim Garland, and many other militant songs, was the daughter of a father blinded in a coal mine and the wife and mother of men killed in the mines.

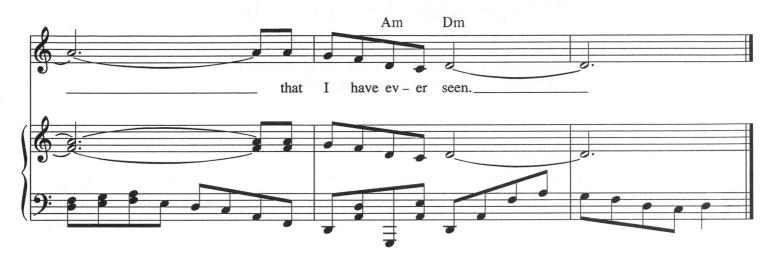

that I have ev – er seen.

Harry Simms was a pal of mine,
We labored side by side,
Expecting to be shot on sight
Or taken for a ride
By some life-stealing gun thug
That roams from town to town
To shoot and kill our union men,
Where e'er they may be found.

Harry Simms and I was parted
At five o'clock that day.
"Be careful, my dear brother,"
To Harry I did say.
"Now I must do my duty,"
Was his reply to me;
"If I get killed by gun thugs
Don't grieve after me."

Harry Simms was walking up the track
That bright sunshiny day.
He was a youth of courage,
His steps was light and gay;
He did not know the gun thugs
Was hiding on the way
To kill our brave young hero
That bright sunshiny day.

Harry Simms was killed on Brush Creek
In nineteen thirty-two;
He organized the miners
Into the NMU;
He gave his life in struggle
'Twas all that he could do;
He died for the union,
He died for me and you.

The thugs can kill our leaders
And cause us to shed tears,
But they cannot kill our spirit
If they try a million years.
We have learned our lesson
Now we all realize
A union struggle must go on
Till we are organized.

Which Side Are You On ?

Florence Reece was the wife of Sam Reece, a union organizer in the coal fields of "bloody" Harlan County, Kentucky. One night in 1931, a band of deputies under High Sheriff J. H. Blair broke into her home. Days later Mrs. Reece wrote the words to "Which Side Are You On?" to the tune of an old Baptist hymn.

Words by Florence Reece

Come all of you good work — ers, good news to you I'll tell, of how the good old un — ion has come in here to dwell

Chorus
Which side are you on? Which side are you on?

Which side are you on? Which side are you on?

Don't scab for the bosses, don't listen to their lies.
Us poor folks haven't got a chance, unless we organize. *Chorus*

They say in Harlan County, there are no neutrals there.
You'll either be a union man, or a thug for J.H. Blair. *Chorus*

Oh, workers, can you stand it? Oh, tell me how you can.
Will you be a lousy scab, or will you be a man? *Chorus*

My daddy was a miner, and I'm a miner's son,
And I'll stick with the union, till every battle's won. *Chorus*

Courtesy of New York Public Library Picture Collection

Solidarity Forever

Ralph Chaplin wrote songs for the International Workers of the World (the "Wobblies"). This was unquestionably the greatest song produced by the American labor movement.

Words by Ralph Chaplin
Tune: John Brown's Body

Sol – i – dar-i–ty for–ev — er, sol – i – dar–i–ty for–ev — er,

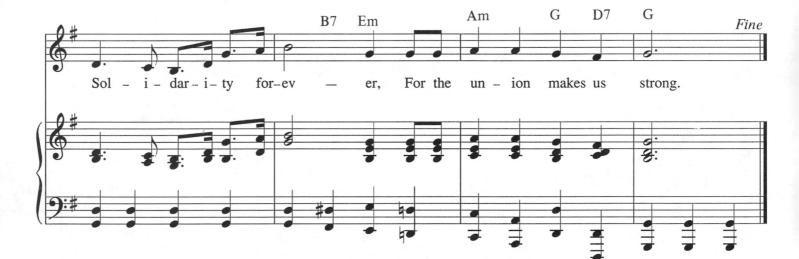

Sol – i – dar–i–ty for-ev — er, For the un – ion makes us strong.

When the un – ion's in – spi – ra – tion through the work – er's blood shall run, There can

be no great-er pow-er an-y-where be-neath the sun; Yet what force on earth is weak-er than the

fee-ble strength of one, For the un-ion makes us strong.

It is we who ploughed the prairies, built the cities where they trade,
Dug the mines and built the workshops, endless miles of railroad laid;
Now we stand outcast and starving 'mid the wonders we have made,
But the union makes us strong. *Chorus*

They have taken untold millions that they never toiled to earn,
But without our brain and muscle not a single wheel can turn;
We can break their haughty power, gain our freedom when we learn
That the union makes us strong. *Chorus*

In our hands is placed a power greater than their hoarded gold,
Greater than the might of atoms magnified a thousandfold;
We can bring to birth a new world from the ashes of the old,
For the union makes us strong. *Chorus*

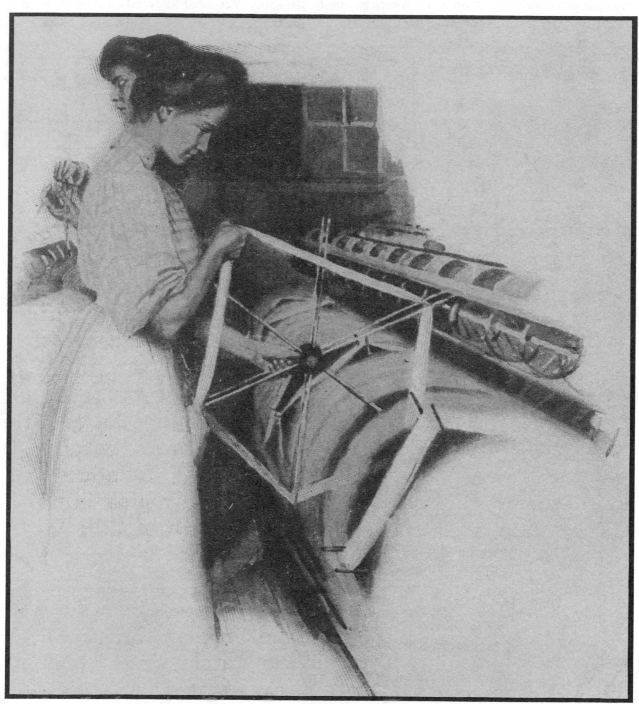

Courtesy of New York Public Library Picture Collection

Work Songs

Winnsboro Cotton Mill Blues

Old man Sar – gent, sit – tin' at the desk, The damned old fool won't
When I die, don't bu – ry me at all, Just hang me up on the

give us no rest.__ He'd take the nick – els off a dead man's eyes To
spool – room wall.__ Just place a knot – ter in my good right hand, So

buy a Co – ca Co – la and an Es – ki – mo Pie.__ I got the blues, I got the
I can keep a – spool – in' in the Prom – ised Land. _

blues, I got the Winns – b'ro Cot – ton Mill blues.__

When I die, don't bury me deep,
Bury me down on 600 Street.
Place a bobbin in each hand,
So I can doff in the promised land. *Chorus*

Drill, Ye Tarriers, Drill

Unskilled and unorganized Irish laborers in the 19th century were subjected to a never-ending stream of indignities.
All that was left to them before the advent of unions was bitter humor expressed in song.

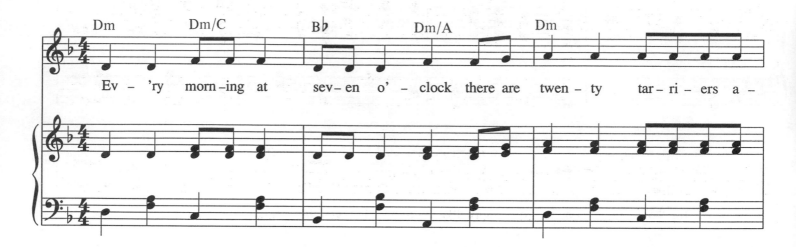

Ev – 'ry morn –ing at sev – en o' – clock there are twen – ty tar – ri – ers a –

work–ing at the rock, And the boss comes a – round and he says, "Keep still! And

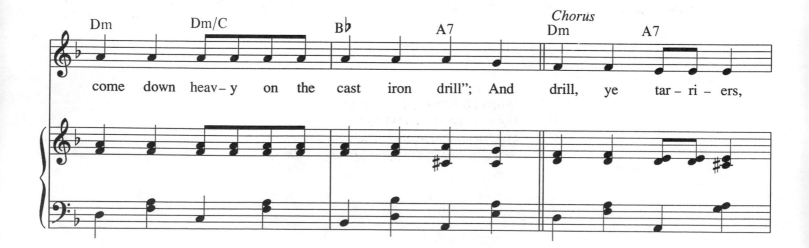

come down heav– y on the cast iron drill"; And drill, ye tar – ri – ers,

Now, our new foreman was Jim McCann,
By God, he was a blame mean man,
Last week a premature blast went off,
And a mile in the air went Big Jim Goff. *Chorus*

The next time payday come around,
Jim Goff a dollar short was found.
When he asked, "What for?" came this reply,
"You're docked for the time you was up in the sky". *Chorus*

Now, the boss was a fine man down to the ground,
And he married a lady six feet round;
She baked good bread and she baked it well,
But she baked it hard as the holes in hell. *Chorus*

John Henry

"John Henry" — the classic battle between man (in this case, a black man) and the machine — can be interpreted as an aphorism for the entire coming of the Industrial Age. Here, man is victorious — but at what price?

Well, — ev – 'ry Mon – day — morn-ing,——————— When the

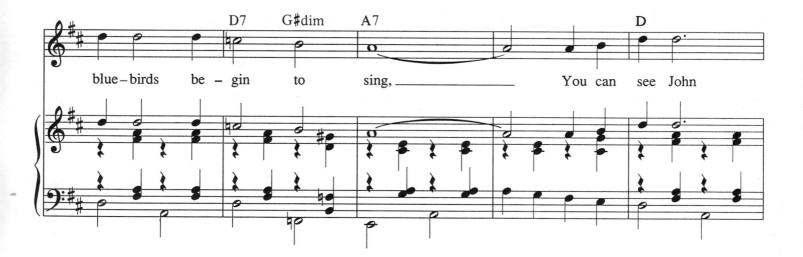

blue – birds be – gin to sing, —————— You can see John

Hen – ry —— out —— on the line. —— You can hear —— John ——

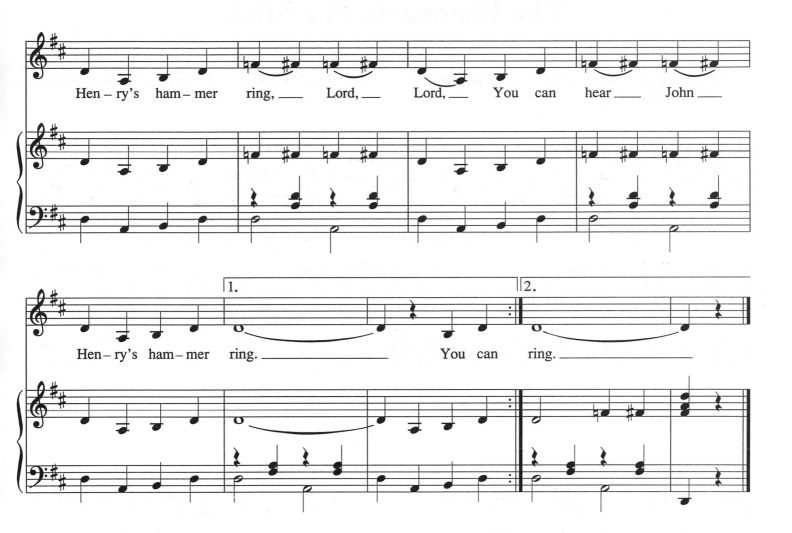

When John Henry was a little baby,
A-sitting on his papa's knee,
He picked up a hammer and a little piece of steel,
Said, "Hammer's gonna be the death of me."   (2)

Well, the captain said to John Henry,
"Gonna bring me a steam drill 'round,
Gonna bring me a steam drill out on the job,
Gonna whup that steel on down."   (2)

John Henry said to his captain,
"A man ain't nothin' but a man,
And before I let that steam drill beat me down,
I'll die with a hammer in my hand."   (2)

John Henry said to his shaker,
"Shaker, why don't you pray?
'Cause if I miss this little piece of steel,
Tomorrow be your buryin' day."   (2)

John Henry was driving on the mountain,
And his hammer was flashing fire,
And the last words I heard that poor boy say,
"Gimme a cool drink of water 'fore I die."   (2)

John Henry, he drove fifteen feet,
The steam drill only made nine.
But he hammered so hard that he broke his poor heart,
And he laid down his hammer and he died.   (2)

They took John Henry to the graveyard
And they buried him in the sand,
And every locomotive comes a-roaring by says,
"There lies a steel-driving man."   (2)

169

The Farmer Is The Man

This song dates from the 1880s, when midwestern farmers first organized and started voting for the Greenback and Populist parties.

When the farm – er comes to town, With his wag – on bro - ken down, } Oh, the
When the law – yer hangs a – round, while the butch – er cuts a pound, }

farm – er is the man who feeds them all. If you'll on – ly look and see I_____
And the preach–er and the cook go a–

think you will a – gree, That the } farm – er is the man who feeds them all. The
stroll – ing by the brook. Oh, the }

farm – er is the man,_____ The farm – er is the man Lives on cred – it till the

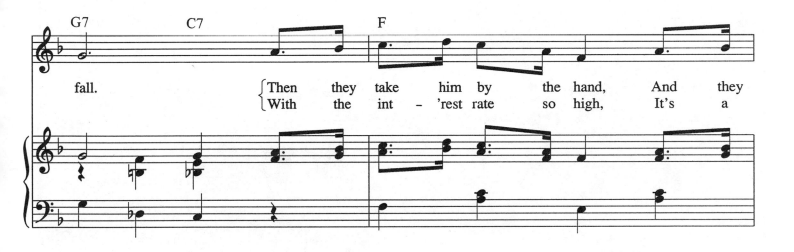

fall. Then they take him by the hand, And they
With the int – 'rest rate so high, It's a

lead him from the land, And the mid – dle–man's the one who gets it all.
won – der he don't die, For the mort– gage man's the one who gets it all.

Courtesy of New York Public Library Picture Collection

The Great Depression 1930s

Evicting sharecroppers. Missouri, 1939

The Panic Is On

The next four songs all deal with various impressions of the Great Depression of the 1930s...people selling apples on the street...trying to make do with little...moving on...saying goodbye to Herbert Hoover and hello to Franklin Delano Roosevelt...

174

Can't on, _____ on. _____

Can't get work, can't draw no pay,
Things are worse, each day.
Nothing to eat, no place to sleep,
All night long folks are walking the street.
   Doggone—I mean the panic is on.

Saw a man this morning, walking down the street,
No shoes on his feet.
You oughta seen the women in their flats,
You could hear 'em saying, "What kinda man is that?"…

All them landlords done raised the rent,
Folks are badly bent.
Where they gets the dough from, goodness knows,
But if they don't produce it—in the street they go…

Some play numbers, some read your mind,
Rackets of all kinds.
Some trimming corns offa people's feet,
They gotta do something to make ends meet…

Some women selling apples, some selling pie,
Selling gin and rye.
Some are selling socks to support their man,
In fact, some are selling everything they can…

I've pawned clothes, pawned my everything,
Pawned my watch and ring.
Pawned my razor but not my gun,
So if luck don't change, there'll be some stealing done…

Old Prohibition's ruined everything,
That's why I must sing.
Here's one thing I want you all to hear:
'Til they bring back light wine, gin and beer,
   Doggone—the panic will be on.

Beans, Bacon And Gravy

Government works projects were instituted to help the unemployed. The WPA (Works Projects Administration) put people to work building roads, post offices and other similar undertakings. Former President Herbert Hoover was held personally responsible by many for the Depression. The term "Hooverized", in the third verse, means "doing without" or substituting something of inferior quality for an all-too-expensive original.

I was born long a – go in eight–een nine–ty four, And I've seen man–y a pan–ic, I will own. I've been hun–gry, I've been cold, and now I'm grow–ing old, But the worst I've seen is nine–teen thir–ty one.

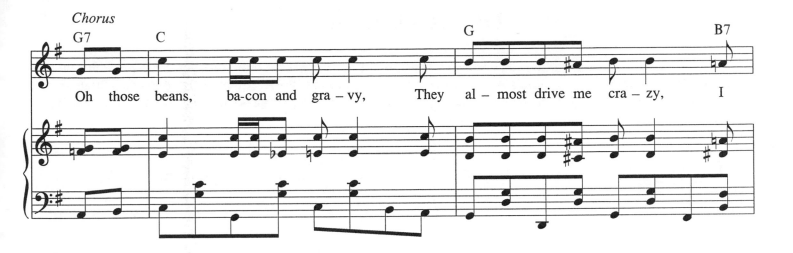

Oh those beans, ba-con and gra-vy, They al — most drive me cra-zy, I

eat them till I see them in my dreams. When I wake up in the morn-ing and a—

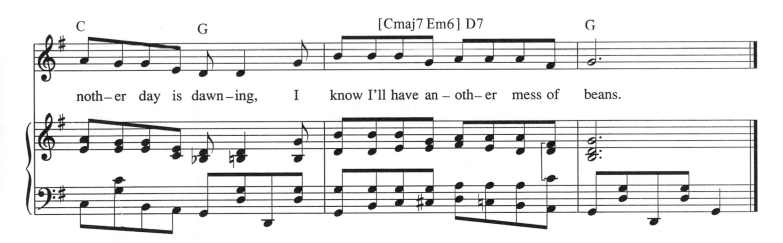

noth-er day is dawn-ing, I know I'll have an-oth-er mess of beans.

We congregate each morning,
At the country barn at dawning,
And everyone is happy so it seems,
But when our work is done,
We file in one by one,
And thank the Lord for one more mess of beans. *Chorus*

We have Hooverized on butter;
For milk we've only water,
And I haven't seen a steak in many a day;
As for pies and cakes and jellies,
We substitute sow-bellies,
For which we work the county road each day. *Chorus*

If there ever comes a time
When I have more than a dime,
They will have to put me under lock and key,
For I've been broke so long
I can only sing this song,
Of the workers and their misery. *Chorus*

Depression Blues

"In that time just about all the men and women was on the WPA. That was the only work you could get at that time and it lasted a long time, too. Louis Armstrong recorded a song called 'WPA,' Casey Bill and Peetie Wheatstraw recorded a 'WPA Blues.' In that time anything you'd say about WPA was all right because that was all you had to live on." (Big Bill Broonzy)

But de — pres — sions has got __ me, some — bo — dy help me,

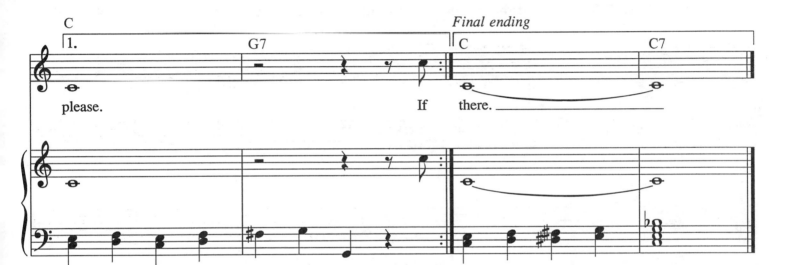

please.   If   there. _____

If I don't feel no better than I feel today,
If I don't feel no better than I feel today,
I'm gonna pack my few clothes and make my
  getaway.

I've begged and I've borrowed till my friends
  don't want me 'round.
I've begged and I've borrowed till my friends
  don't want me 'round.
I'll take old man Depression and leave this
  no-good town.

Depression's here, they tell me it's everywhere;
Depression's here, they tell me it's everywhere;
So I'm going back to Florida and see if Depression's there.

White House Blues

Roosevelt's in the White House, doing his best,
While old Hoover is layin' around and takin' his rest,
Now he's gone I'm glad he's gone!

Pants all busted, patches all way down,
People got so ragged, they couldn't go to town,
Now he's gone, I'm glad he's gone!

Workin' in the coal mines, twenty cents a ton,
Fourteen long hours and your work day is done,
Now he's gone, I'm glad he's gone!

People all angry, they all got the blues,
Wearing patched britches and old tennis shoes,
Now he's gone I'm glad he's gone!

Got up this morning, all I could see
Was corn bread and gravy just a-waitin' for me,
And now he's gone, I'm glad he's gone!

Look here, Mr. Hoover, and see what you done,
You went off a-fishin', let the country go to ruin,
Now he's gone, I'm glad he's gone!

Fort Bragg, 1941

World War II
1939–1945

Courtesy of New York Public Library Picture Collection

Draftee's Blues

The blues is a perfect vehicle with which a soldier may express his feelings. Any number of verses can be added on - the personal, the humorous and the serious.

When you look in–to your mail–box and you find your ques–tion–aire,

When you look in–to your mail–box and you

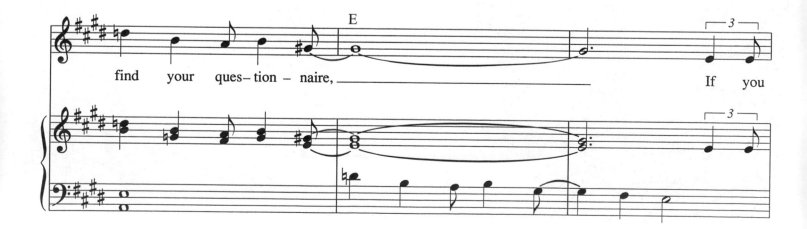

find your ques–tion – naire, _____ If you

pass   your 'xam – in – a – tion –   won't   noth – in' help   you   but   pray –

er. _____   They will _____

They will take you to the depot and put you on the train,
Yes, they'll take you to the depot — put you on the train,
And the Good Lord only knows if you'll be comin' home again.

You may be mean as a lion, you may be gentle as a lamb,
You may be mean as a lion — gentle as a lamb,
Just take your mind off your wife and put it on Uncle Sam.

They will train you with a rifle — Lord, with a hand grenade,
They will train you with a rifle — Lord, with a hand grenade,
So when you meet that Nazi, man, you won't be afraid.

I want all of you draftees to put your mind on your training camp,
I want all of you draftees to put your mind on your training camp,
So when you meet old Hitler, your powder won't be damp.

I want to tell you women just as easy as I can,
I want to tell all you women — easy as I can,
Uncle Sam ain't no woman but he sure can take your man.

Gee But I Wanna Go Home

This is a World War I song updated to World War II.

The coffee that they give you, they say is mighty fine,
It's good for cuts and bruises, And it tastes like i-o-dine.

Chorus

I don't want no more of army life, gee, but I wanna go home.

The biscuits that they give you they say are mighty fine;
One rolled off a table and it killed a pal of mine.
Chorus

The chickens that they give you they say are mighty fine;
One rolled off a table and it started marking time.
Chorus

The details that they give us they say are mighty fine;
The garbage that we pick up they feed us all the time.
Chorus

The clothes that they give you they say are mighty fine;
But me and my buddy can both fit into mine.
Chorus

The women in the service club they say are mighty fine,
But most are over ninety and the rest are under nine.
Chorus

They treat us all like monkeys and make us stand in line;
They give you fifty dollars and take back forty-nine.
Chorus

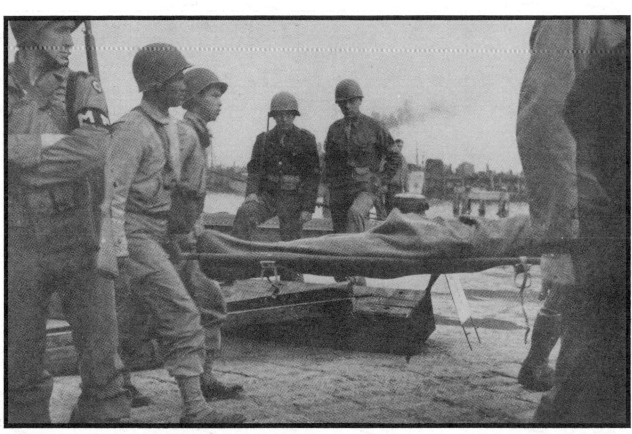

Courtesy of New York Public Library Picture Collection

'Round and Around Hitler's Grave

The old fiddle tune "Old Joe Clark" served as the basis for this optimistic assessment of the progress of the war.

I'm a - go - ing o - ver - seas, tell you what I'll do. I'll

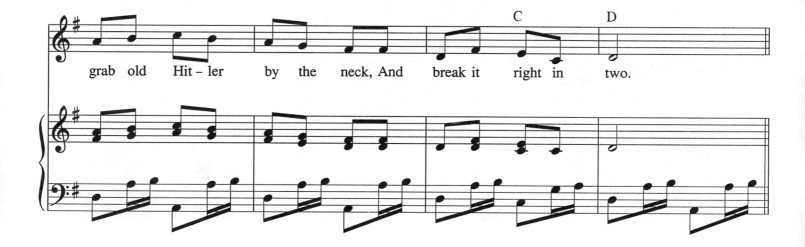

grab old Hit - ler by the neck, And break it right in two.

Chorus

'Round and a - round Hit - ler's grave, 'Round and a - round we go, We're

188

gon - na lay that poor boy down; He won't get up no more.

Hitler he bombed London,
It was a mighty blitz;
But after we get through with him,
We'll give that poor boy fits.   *Chorus*

Hitler said the Third Reich
Would last a thousand years.
His tanks are rolling backwards now—
We've made him strip his gears.   *Chorus*

Goebbels said to Goering,
"We're in an awful fix,
The Yanks are dropping ten-ton bombs—
Berlin's a pile of bricks."   *Chorus*

They marched right into Russia,
Just like Napoleon.
But when the snows began to fall,
They knew their time had come.   *Chorus*

If anyone should ask you
Who was it sang this song,
It was a G.I. soldier boy,
As he does march along.   *Chorus*

United Nations Make A Chain

As World War II drew to a close, the people of the world had a vision of a lasting peace to be guaranteed by the United Nations. So far, things have not worked out quite the way we would have liked. The tune for this song comes from the spiritual "Hold On."

U — nit — ed na — tions make a chain, Ev — 'ry link is free — dom's name, Keep your hand on __ that plow, hold on. __ Hold on, _____ hold on, _____ keep your

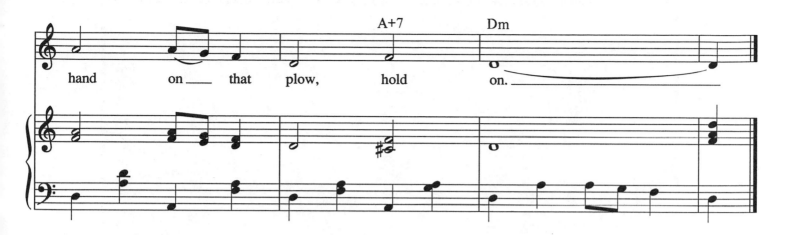

Now the war is over and done,
Let's keep that peace that we have won;
Keep your hand on that plow, hold on!   *Chorus*

Freedom's name is mighty sweet;
Black and white are gonna meet;
Keep your hand on that plow, hold on!   *Chorus*

Many men have fought and died
So we could be here side by side;
Keep your hand on that plow, hold on!   *Chorus*

Courtesy of New York Public Library Picture Collection

The Korean War
1950–1953

Courtesy of New York Public Library Picture Collection

Rotation Blues

During the Korean War (1950-53) American soldiers who accumulated a certain number of points by taking part in combat were rotated from the front lines to positions in the rear. This song was inspired by the first few lines penned by a lonely G.I. up front.

Music and Additional Words by
Jerry Silverman

This rain in Korea sure is cold and wet,
This rain in Korea sure is cold and wet,
These rotation papers sure are hard to get.
    I got the ro-ro-ta-tion blues.

If I ever live to be, what you call, a thirty-year man,
Live to be a thirty-year man,
And my luck holds out—be rotated back to Japan.
    I got the ro-ro-ta-tion blues.

If I could just sit down and rest a while, nothin' would be finer,
Yes—nothin' would be finer,
It seems like we've been walking all the way to China.
    I got the ro-ro-ta-tion blues.

A two-week leave in Japan sure would be great,
A two-week leave in Japan sure would be great,
But Japan is still a million miles from the Golden Gate.
    I got the ro-ro-ta-tion blues.

195

The Dying Soldier

Al Wood flew a bomber in World War II. Here he expresses his thoughts about the futility of war.

By Albert Wood

Now I lay me down to die, I ask you ma – ma, please don't cry. My small tin sol – diers just passed through, And mom, your son went march – ing, too. With

With Jack and Jill we climbed the hill,
Guess we took an awful spill.
All of us came tumbling down,
And here am I upon the ground.

Tom, Tom, the piper's son,
Picked up Jack and away did run.
He looked at me and shook his head,
And lay me on the side instead.

Humpty-Dumpty and King Cole,
Sat around and counted their gold.
They made a profit off the toys,
That are killing the little boys.

To last verse

Last verse

Miss Bo Peep is seek–ing her sheep, From night un–til the dawn.

Ma – ma, ma – ma, hold me tight – Boy Blue has come to blow his horn.

The Ghost Army Of Korea

This is a British Army song that was picked up by the American G.I.s serving in Korea.

Just be-low the Man-chu-ri-an bor-der,_____ Ko-re-a's the
name of the spot,_____ We're due to be spend-ing our time here,_____
In the land_____ that God_____ for-got._____

Down with the snakes and the lizards,
Down where a swaddie is blue,
Right in the middle of nowhere,
And thousands of miles from you.

We sweat and we freeze and we shiver.
It's more than a man can bear.
We're not a bunch of convicts
We're only doing our share.

We're soldiers in the army,
Earning our measly pay,
Guarding all the millionaires
For four lousy shillings a day.

Living with photos and mem'ries,
Thinking sometimes of our gals.
Hoping that while we have been away,
They have not married our pals.

Few people know what we are doing,
And nobody gives a damn.
Although we are almost forgotten,
We belong to the khaki clan.

The good times we've had in the army,
And the good times we have missed,
Here's hoping the army don't get you
So for God's sake don't go and enlist.

And when we arrive up in heaven,
St. Peter will surely tell,
"They've just come back from Korea, dear God,
They've been serving their time in hell."

The Vietnam War
1964–1975

Courtesy of New York Public Library Picture Collection

Taisau (Why)

"This song has nothing to do with the war — it simply deals with what every type of serviceman does and thinks about when he's not fighting: girls and beer. This was true in the wars before this one and it will always be true. There are some Vietnamese words in the song. 'Taisau' is a question that is on the lips of most Americans, 'why?' 'Taivu' is our answer, 'because.' 'Co dep' is a pretty girl and 'bamuyba' is the type of beer they drink. The expression 'too much' is very popular in Viet Nam — they never say 'very.' We spent many hours together singing this song and it sure helped when we were feeling low. . . ." (Written in Viet Nam by Lance Corporal Ralph Columbino, USMC)

"Tai - sau,___ tai - sau,''___ said she ___ to me. "Tal - vi,___ tai -

vi,''___ said I. _____ Sai - gon to - mor - row, to - night I'm in

Hue. If the V. C. don't get me we'll say that's one day.

I went to a bar 'way down by the track,
There stood a "co dep" - long hair down her back;
Her eyes, how they sparkled in response to my touch.
I told her I loved her, I loved her too much.   *Chorus*

Hey you, come in, sit down, what your name?
How long have you been in Viet Nam?
I've been in your country the whole live-long day,
So sit right down right by me and hear what I say.   *Chorus*

I'm tired of drinking your old "bamuyba",
I'm tired of fighting your old war.
I'm packing my bags and I'm going back home
To my sweet little Vickie, the girl I adore.   *Chorus*

Courtesy of New York Public Library Picture Collection

Every Day

Words and music by an anonymous American soldier, a prisoner of war in North Vietnam. It was transcribed from the soldier's singing as heard on a radio broadcast from Hanoi Radio.

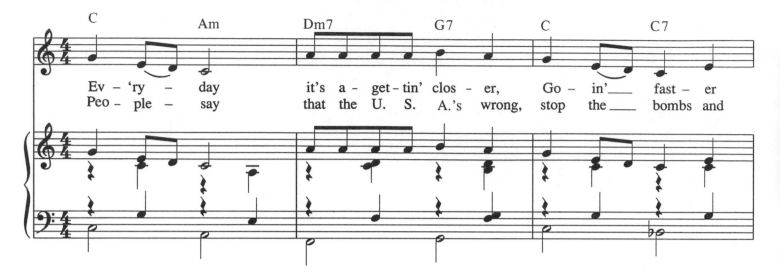

Ev – 'ry – day   it's a – get – tin' clos – er,   Go – in'___ fast – er
Peo – ple – say   that the U. S. A.'s wrong, stop the ___ bombs and

than a rol – ler coast – er,   A move to end the ___ war has ___
bring all the G. I.s home,   For soon an end to the war will ___

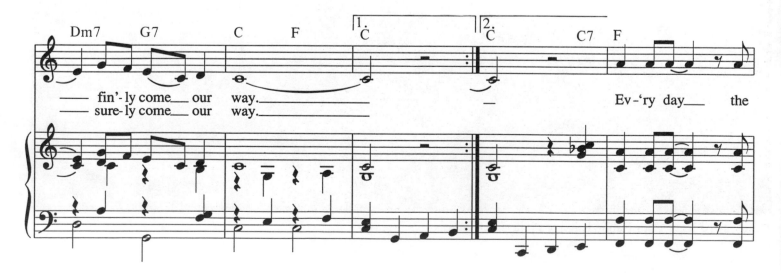

___ fin' – ly come ___ our way. ___
___ sure – ly come ___ our way. ___   Ev –'ry day ___ the

move ment's get- tin' strong – er, Ev'– ry way___ just a lit- tle strong- er, the

U. S. A.___ all the peo-ple long for an end to war.

Ev-'ry – day peo-ple are cry – in; End the war,___ stop the need -less dy – in;___

___ An end to the war will___ sure-ly come - our way.___

203

Courtesy of New York Public Library Picture Collection

The Civil Rights
Movement
1960s

Courtesy of New York Public Library Picture Collection

Woke Up This Morning
With My Mind On Freedom

Reverend Osby of Aurora, Illinois, made up this revamp of the old gospel song "I Woke Up This Morning with My Mind on Jesus" in the Hinds County (Mississippi) jail during the Freedom rides in 1961. In mid-March 1961, the Congress of Racial Equality began sending bi-racial groups to ride Greyhound and Trailways buses from Washington, D.C., to New Orleans, with the purpose of challenging any segregation of interstate travellers.

206

free – dom, Hal-le - lu, Hal-le -lu, Hal-le - lu, Ha-le-lu, Hal-le - lu – ia.

Walk, walk, ___ walk, walk, ___ Walk, walk, ___ with my mind on free - dom, ___

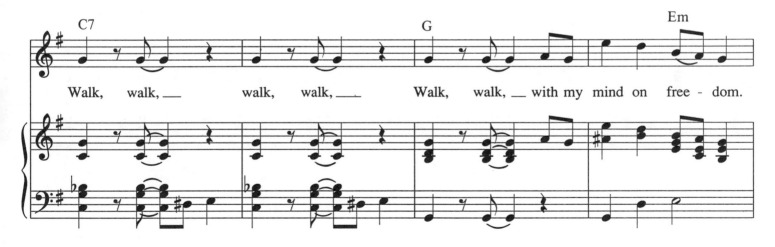

Walk, walk, ___ walk, walk, ___ Walk, walk, ___ with my mind on free - dom.

Ah, ___ ah ___ Walk, walk, ___ walk, walk. ___

Freedom Train A-Comin'

The civil rights movement singers were good at borrowing and adapting traditional melodies and setting new words to them. This song is an adaptation of the old union song "Union Train."

Oh, hear___ that free ___ dom train a – com–in', com–in',

com–in',Oh, hear___ that free ___ dom train a com–in', com–in',

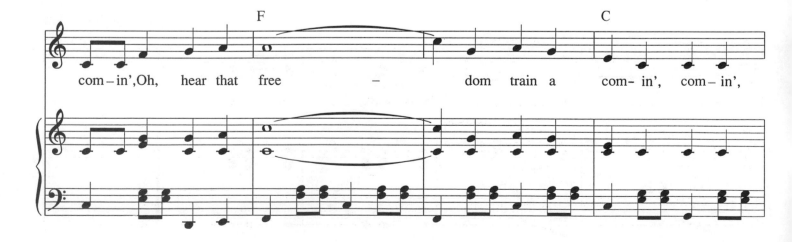

com–in',Oh, hear that free ___ dom train a com–in', com–in',

com – in', Get on board, _____ get on board. _____

It'll be carryin' nothing but freedom, freedom, freedom. (3)
   Get on board, get on board.

They'll be comin' by the thousand, thousand, thousand. (3)
   Get on board, get on board.

It'll be carryin' freedom fighters, fighters, fighters. (3)
   Get on board, get on board.

It'll be carryin' registered voters, voters, voters. (3)
   Get on board, get on board.

It'll be rollin' through Mississippi, Mississippi. (3)
   Get on board, get on board.

Repeat first verse

Free At Last

"When we let freedom ring, when we let it ring from every village and every hamlet, from every state and every city, we will be able to speed up that day when all of God's children, black men and white men, Jews and Gentiles, Protestants and Catholics, will be able to join hands and sing in the words of the old Negro spiritual, 'Free at last! Free at last! Thank God almighty, we are free at last!' " (Martin Luther King, "I Have a Dream" speech, 1963)

Free at last, free at last, I thank God I'm

free at last; Free at last, free at last,_____

I thank God I'm free at last. Oh, free at last.

Way down yon–der in the grave–yard walk, I thank God I'm free at last,

Me and my Je–sus gon–na meet and talk,___ I thank God I'm free at last. Oh,

On my knees when the light passed by,
I thank God I'm free at last,
Thought my soul would rise and fly,
I thank God I'm free at last. *Chorus*

Some of these mornings, bright and fair,
I thank God I'm free at last,
Gonna meet my Jesus in the middle of the air,
I thank God I'm free at last. *Chorus*

Freedom Is A Constant Struggle

"In this summer the stranger is the enemy, and the men of Mississippi wait and watch for him. In khaki pants and straw hat they stand their watch against the civil rights workers across the Delta counties. By night they ride dipping roads in the hill country to the east where that fatal plant, the kudzu vine, grows everywhere strangling grass and tree. Along Route 19 they drive through Neshoba County's scrub oak and scraggly pine forests without headlights when the moon is bright and the mist is sparse and patchy. For the Negroes, fear makes the night wakeful. Negro farmers check their guns and count their children as the night comes on. The short nights of summer are long — longer than ever now because the white civil rights workers are living hidden among the Negro farm folk." (Nicholas Von Hoffman, *Mississippi Notebook,* 1964)

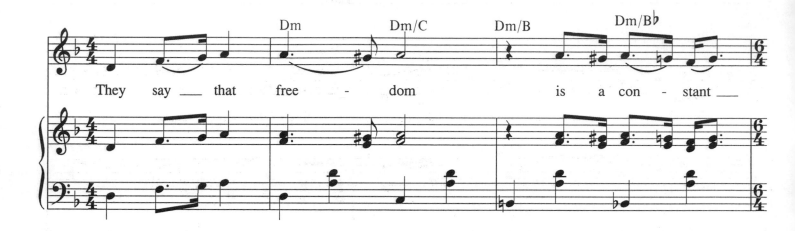

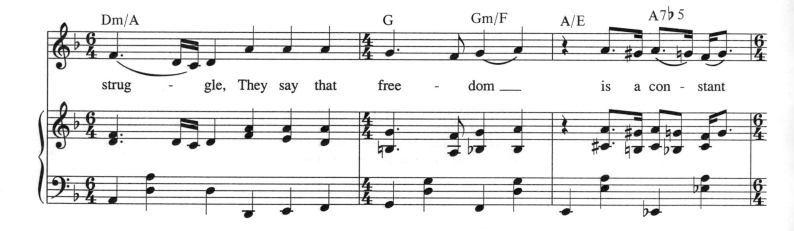

They say that freedom is a constant crying . . . (3)
Oh Lord, we've cried so long,
We must be free, we must be free.

They say that freedom is a constant sorrow . . . (3)
Oh Lord, we've sorrowed so long,
We must be free, we must be free.

They say that freedom is a constant moaning . . . (3)
Oh Lord, we've moaned so long,
We must be free, we must be free.

They say that freedom is a constant dying . . . (3)
Oh Lord, we've died so long.
We must be free, we must be free.

Courtesy of New York Public Library Picture Collection

Campaigns
and
Campaigners

GEN. U.S. GRANT FOR PRESIDENT.

NATIONAL UNION REPUBLICAN CANDIDATES

HON. SCHUYLER COLFAX FOR VICE PRESIDENT

Courtesy of New York Public Library Picture Collection

Election-The Peoples' Right

Standing above later partisan election campaign songs is this hymn-like song dedicated to the fundamental principle of our country - the right of free elections.

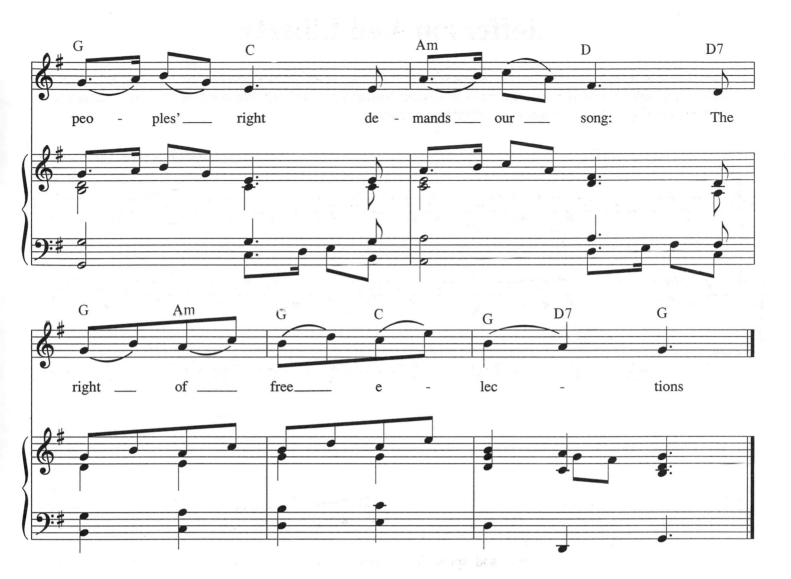

peo - ples'___ right de - mands___ our___ song: The

right ___ of ___ free___ e - lec - tions

For government and order's sake,
And law's important sections,
Let's all stand by the ballot box,
For freedom of elections. *Chorus*

Each town and county's wealth and peace,
Its trade and all connections,
With science, arts must all increase,
By fair and free elections. *Chorus*

Then thwart the schemes of fighting lands
And traitor disaffections,
Stand up with willing heart and hands,
For fair and free elections. *Chorus*

Should enemies beset us round
Of foreign fierce complexions,
Undaunted we can stand our ground,
Upheld by free elections. *Chorus*

Elections are to make us laws
For trade, peace and protection,
Who fails to vote forsakes the cause
Of fair and free elections. *Chorus*

Jefferson And Liberty

This song was written after Jefferson's election in 1801. The "reign of terror" mentioned in the first verse refers to the Adams administration's Alien and Sedition Laws, which had led to a period of political inquisition, with a restriction on freedom of speech and the arrests of newspaper editors.

Words by Robert Treat Paine, Jr.

join with heart and soul _ and voice for _ Jef - fer - son _ and lib - er - ty.

O'er vast Columbia's varied clime,
Her cities, forests, shores and dales,
In rising majesty sublime,
Immortal Liberty prevails.   *Chorus*

Hail, long expected, glorious day!
Illustrious, memorable morn,
That Freedom's fabric from decay
Rebuilds, for millions yet unborn. *Chorus*

His country's surest hope and stay,
In virtue and in talents tried,
Now rises to assume the sway,
O'er Freedom's Temple to preside. *Chorus*

Within its hallowed walls immense,
No hireling Bands shall e'er arise,
Arrayed in Tyranny's defense,
To crush an injured people's cries. *Chorus*

No Lordling here, with gorging jaws,
Shall wring from Industry its food;
Nor fiery bigots' Holy Laws
Lay waste our fields and streets in blood. *Chorus*

Here Strangers from a thousand shores,
Compelled by Tyranny to roam,
Shall find, amidst abundant stores,
A nobler and a happier home.   *Chorus*

Here Art shall lift her laureled head,
Wealth, Industry and Peace divine,
And where dark pathless Forests spread,
Rich fields and lofty cities shine. *Chorus*

From Europe's wants and woes remote,
A dreary waste of waves between,
Here plenty cheers the humblest cot,
And smiles on every Village Green. *Chorus*

Here, free as air's expanded space,
To every soul and sect shall be
The sacred priv'lege of our race,
The Worship of the Deity.   *Chorus*

These gifts, great Liberty, are thine;
Ten thousand more we owe to thee
Immortal may their mem'ries shine
Who fought and died for Liberty. *Chorus*

What heart but hails a scene so bright,
What soul but inspiration draws,
Who would not guard so dear a right,
Or die in such a glorious cause? *Chorus*

Let Foes to Freedom dread the name,
But should they touch the sacred Tree,
Twice fifty thousand swords shall flame
For Jefferson and Liberty. *Chorus*

From Georgia to Lake Champlain,
From seas to Mississippi's shore,
The Sons of Freedom loud proclaim,
The Reign of Terror now is o'er. *Chorus*

Lincoln and Liberty

From the *Hutchinson Republican Songster* for the campaign of 1860. Jesse Hutchinson picked a sure-fire, often-used, well-known tune, the Irish song "Rosin the Beau," to help sweep Abraham Lincoln into office. Hutchinson drew upon the migrations of the Lincoln family to instill a sense of "native son" pride in the voters of three states: Lincoln was born in Kentucky, his family lived in Indiana from 1816 to 1830, and his political career was based in Illinois (whose citizens were known as "Suckers").

Words by Jesse Hutchinson

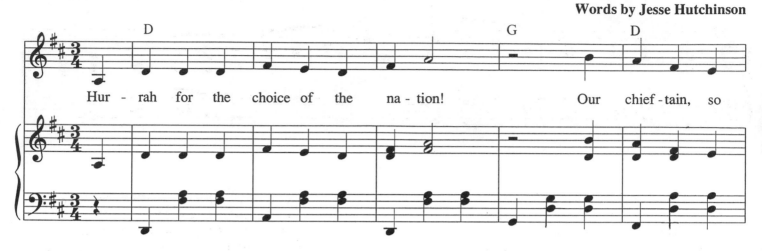

Hur - rah for the choice of the na - tion! Our chief - tain, so

brave and so true; _____ We'll go for the great Re - form - a - tion,

For Lin - coln and Li - ber - ty too!_____ We'll go for the

son of Ken - tuck - y, _____ The he - ro of Hoo - sier - dom

through; _____ The pride of the Suck - ers so luck - y, For

Lin - coln and Lib - er - ty too, _____ Our too! _____

They'll find what by felling and mauling
Our railmaker statesman can do;
For the people are every where calling
For Lincoln and Liberty too.
Then up with the banner so glorious,
The star-spangled red, white, and blue,
We'll fight till our banner's victorious,
For Lincoln and Liberty, too.

Our David's good sling is unerring,
The Slavocrat's giant he slew,
Then shout for the freedom preferring,
For Lincoln and Liberty, too.
We'll go for the son of Kentucky,
The hero of Hoosierdom through,
The pride of the "Suckers" so lucky,
For Lincoln and Liberty, too.

A-Smoking His Cigar

Simon Bolivar Buckner, the commander of Fort Donelson, Tennessee, the besieged Confederate outpost on the Cumberland River, sent a proposal to attacking General Ulysses S. Grant for the discussion of surrender terms. Grant had the Fort hemmed in on three sides, and Flag Officer Andrew Foote had his Union gunboats on the river facing the Fort. Grant's reply: "No terms except an unconditional and immediate surrender can be accepted." In 1868, when Grant was running for President, this victory inspired the following song.

Words by "Ason O'Fagun"
Music by J. P. Webster

At Don - el - son the reb - el horde had gath - ered in their
And Beau — re - gard did swear, me thinks, Up — on his bend - ed

might, De - ter - mined there with fire and sword to
knee, That his good horse should have some drinks, All

make a dread - ful fight; But gal - lant Foote with
from the Ten — nes — see; But ah! a "slip twixt

his com-mand Went in by wat - er route, While
cup and lip" that sweet il - lu - sion broke; For

Grant be-sieged up-on the land, And smoked the reb-els out. Where
Grant just smote 'em thigh and hip, And made the reb-els smoke.

vol-leyed thun-der __ loud-est pealed, A-long the front of war, The

Gen'-ral calm-ly viewed the field, A-smok-ing his ci-gar.

The doughty Pem, at Vicksburg, too,
   Did naught of Yankees fear;
Grant passed his guns in quick review,
   And gained the city's rear.
He pitched his tent, deployed his force,
   And lighted his cigar;
Said he, "Misguided lads, of course
   You know just where you are." *Chorus*

And now, let politicians wait,
   There's work for men to do;
We'll place one in the Chair of State
   Who wears the army blue;
The people know just what they want —
   Less TALK, and no more WAR —
FOR PRESIDENT, ULYSSES GRANT,
   A-SMOKING his CIGAR! *Chorus*

Hooray for Bill McKinley
and That Brave Rough Rider, Ted

1900, William McKinley and Theodore Roosevelt *versus* William Jennings Bryant and Adlai Stevenson. In ragtime!

Things are wear-ing a warm com-plex-ion, But Mc-Kin-ley's a-going to
When the great Span-ish war was pend-ing, And the coun-try was all gone

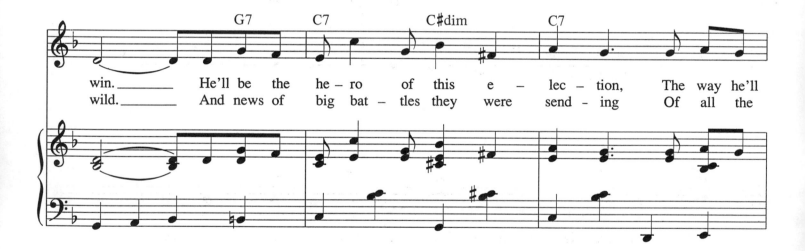

win. _____ He'll be the he-ro of this e-lec-tion, The way he'll
wild. _____ And news of big bat-tles they were send-ing Of all the

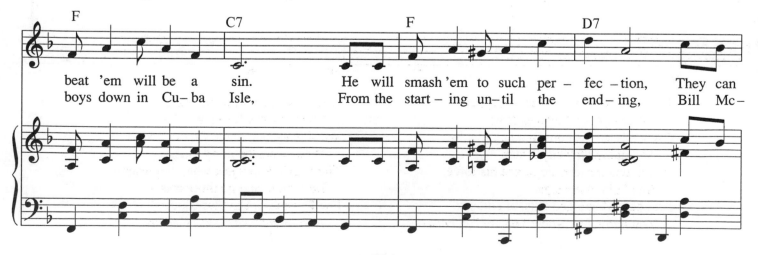

beat 'em will be a sin. He will smash 'em to such per-fec-tion, They can
boys down in Cu-ba Isle, From the start-ing un-til the end-ing, Bill Mc-

226

cer-tain-ly is too a-mus-ing to see those Dem-mies a-trying to sing. But when
rad - ing with torch-lights blaz-ing, A-hail-ing, good-times for Un - cle Sam And when

ev-'ry thing__ is ex - cite-ment, And that good old el-ec-tion's won, And 'tis
ev-er I __ meet a Dem-mie, I don't care if he kills me

count-ed up, good old Mac and Ted-dy will have beat 'em six-teen to one. Oh, then

dead, I'll yell, "Hoo-ray for Bill Mc-Kin-ley and that brave Rough Rid-er, Ted!"

227

Franklin D. Roosevelt's Back Again

In 1936, Roosevelt was running for his second term. The nation was emerging from the Depression. Prohibition (of the sale of alcoholic beverages) had been repealed. Roosevelt was really the people's choice. The "old Martin," in the first verse, is the brand name of a guitar.

I'll take a drink of brandy and let myself be handy,
Good old times are coming back again;
You can laugh and tell a joke, you can dance and drink and smoke,
We've got Franklin D. Roosevelt back again.

Second Chorus:
Back again (back again), back again (back again),
We've got Franklin D. Roosevelt back again.
We'll have money in our jeans, we can travel with the queen,
We've got Franklin D. Roosevelt back again.

No more breadlines we're glad to say, the donkey won election day.
No more standing in the blowing, snowing rain;
He's got things in full sway, we're all working and getting our pay,
We've got Franklin D. Roosevelt back again.
    (First Chorus)

Alphabetical Song Index

Credits

Pages 163, 173, 181, 182: *The Depression Years as Photographed by Arthur Rothstein* is a new work, first published by Dover Publications, Inc., in 1978. Used with permission.

Courtesy of New York Public Library Picture Collection

Great Music at Your Fingertips